Mammals

Patricia Daniels

NATIONAL GEOGRAPHIC
WASHINGTON, D.C.

Contents

WEST INDIAN MANATEE p. 132

OCELOT p. 100

EASTERN GRAY SQUIRREL p. 19

PALLID BAT p. 93

MOOSE p. 134

LET'S LOOK AT
Mammals

RED FOXES LIKE THIS BABY, OR KIT, LIVE IN FORESTS, SUBURBS, AND CITIES ACROSS NORTH AMERICA (SEE PAGE 105).

I HAVE ALWAYS ENJOYED WATCHING MAMMALS. As a child, I spent summers in my backyard in New York watching Gray Squirrels. Some even built a nest between my basketball backboard and the garage! Now, in my home in Utah, I often meander on foot and bicycle around Antelope Island State Park, which lies in Great Salt Lake. Here I periodically pause to observe Coyotes, Pronghorn Antelope, Mule Deer, and Bison— it is a mammal watcher's paradise!

Antelope Island is exactly the kind of place where the *National Geographic Kids Ultimate Explorer Field Guide: Mammals* will be a valuable tool for mammal watchers. Not only in Utah, but across North America, this guide will help readers learn about the amazing range and terrific diversity of mammals that live in our vast continent. Filled with details about their natural history, this guide also contains outstanding photographs of these species. You'll find drawings of their tracks, too, which will enable you to identify mammals without actually seeing them.

Included in this guide are two of North America's more unusual species: the continent's only marsupial, or pouched mammal, the Virginia Opossum; and the sole member of a group that is otherwise found only in Central and South America: the Nine-Banded Armadillo. Other species include tiny, sometimes teacup-size insectivores like the Masked Shrew; burrowers like the Star-Nosed Mole; graceful fliers like the Big Brown Bat; hoofed beauties like the Bison and Wild Horse; and awesome, oceangoing swimmers like the Humpback Whale.

Those who live in or visit this country are lucky when it comes to viewing these mammals. Although many are difficult to see in the wild, many others are easy to observe. To a great degree, this is the result of the continent's large number of protected areas, such as state and national parks. Especially in the western United States, these sanctuaries harbor majestic species such as Elk and wolves, which can be viewed from safe distances—preferably using binoculars and this guide! Enjoy this useful resource as you discover these and more amazing mammals.

Dr. Sam Zeveloff,
Presidential Distinguished Professor Emeritus of Zoology,
Weber State University

HOW TO USE This Book

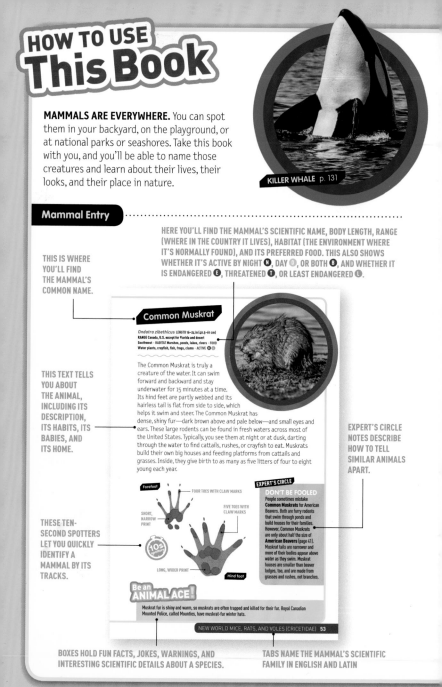

MAMMALS ARE EVERYWHERE. You can spot them in your backyard, on the playground, or at national parks or seashores. Take this book with you, and you'll be able to name those creatures and learn about their lives, their looks, and their place in nature.

KILLER WHALE p. 131

Mammal Entry

THIS IS WHERE YOU'LL FIND THE MAMMAL'S COMMON NAME.

HERE YOU'LL FIND THE MAMMAL'S SCIENTIFIC NAME, BODY LENGTH, RANGE (WHERE IN THE COUNTRY IT LIVES), HABITAT (THE ENVIRONMENT WHERE IT'S NORMALLY FOUND), AND ITS PREFERRED FOOD. THIS ALSO SHOWS WHETHER IT'S ACTIVE BY NIGHT **N**, DAY **D**, OR BOTH **B**, AND WHETHER IT IS ENDANGERED **E**, THREATENED **T**, OR LEAST ENDANGERED **L**.

Common Muskrat

Ondatra zibethicus LENGTH 16–24 in (40.5–61 cm)
RANGE Canada, U.S. except for Florida and desert
Southwest · HABITAT Marshes, ponds, lakes, rivers · FOOD
Water plants, crayfish, fish, frogs, clams · ACTIVE **N** **B**

THIS TEXT TELLS YOU ABOUT THE ANIMAL, INCLUDING ITS DESCRIPTION, ITS HABITS, ITS BABIES, AND ITS HOME.

The Common Muskrat is truly a creature of the water. It can swim forward and backward and stay underwater for 15 minutes at a time. Its hind feet are partly webbed and its hairless tail is flat from side to side, which helps it swim and steer. The Common Muskrat has dense, shiny fur—dark brown above and pale below—and small eyes and ears. These large rodents can be found in fresh waters across most of the United States. Typically, you see them at night or at dusk, darting through the water to find cattails, rushes, or crayfish to eat. Muskrats build their own big houses and feeding platforms from cattails and grasses. Inside, they give birth to as many as five litters of four to eight young each year.

EXPERT'S CIRCLE NOTES DESCRIBE HOW TO TELL SIMILAR ANIMALS APART.

Forefoot

FOUR TOES WITH CLAW MARKS

FIVE TOES WITH CLAW MARKS

SHORT, NARROW PRINT

LONG, WIDER PRINT

Hind foot

THESE TEN-SECOND SPOTTERS LET YOU QUICKLY IDENTIFY A MAMMAL BY ITS TRACKS.

EXPERT'S CIRCLE

DON'T BE FOOLED
People sometimes mistake **Common Muskrats** for American Beavers. Both are furry rodents that swim through ponds and build houses for their families. However, Common Muskrats are only about half the size of **American Beavers** [page 41]. Muskrat tails are narrower and more of their bodies appear above water as they swim. Muskrat houses are smaller than beaver lodges, too, and are made from grasses and rushes, not branches.

Be an ANIMAL ACE!

Muskrat fur is shiny and warm, so muskrats are often trapped and killed for their fur. Royal Canadian Mounted Police, called Mounties, have muskrat-fur winter hats.

NEW WORLD MICE, RATS, AND VOLES (CRICETIDAE) 53

BOXES HOLD FUN FACTS, JOKES, WARNINGS, AND INTERESTING SCIENTIFIC DETAILS ABOUT A SPECIES.

TABS NAME THE MAMMAL'S SCIENTIFIC FAMILY IN ENGLISH AND LATIN

SPECIAL SECTIONS CALLED "MAMMAL MANIA" give you a closer look at unique aspects of mammal life. They'll tell you about hibernation, mammal defenses, creatures in the city, and more.

A CAPTION DESCRIBES THE MAIN PICTURE.

A LARGE TEXT BLOCK GIVES YOU GENERAL INFORMATION.

SHORTER TEXT TELLS YOU ABOUT PARTICULAR ANIMALS.

FOR YOUR SAFETY

While locating animals in their natural habitat can be loads of fun, wild animals can be unpredictable and dangerous. This book is about mammal-watching and is not intended to encourage interaction with wild animals. You should never touch or get too close to a wild animal, as wild animals can carry disease, and can respond erratically. Readers should have their parent's permission before undertaking the activities suggested in this book and be accompanied by a trusted and responsible adult.

Even though this book is packed with useful advice, there is no guarantee that the advice will work in any specific situation. All content and information published in this book is provided to the reader "as is" and without any war- ranties. The situations and activities described in the book carry inherent risks and hazards and should be evaluated before undertaking them. The author and publisher specifically disclaim all responsibility for any liability, loss, or risk, personal or otherwise, incurred as a consequence of the use of the contents in this book.

WHAT IS A Mammal?

THE SQUIRREL DASHING ACROSS YOUR YARD, THE DOLPHIN LEAPING OUT OF THE OCEAN, AND THE PERSON LOOKING BACK AT YOU IN THE MIRROR ARE ALL MAMMALS. Mammals span a wide range of shapes and sizes, from the Kitti's Hog-nosed Bat, no bigger than a bumblebee, to the 100-foot (30.5-m)-long Blue Whale. Mammals walk, fly, dig, jump, climb, and run—some as fast as a speeding car. No wonder these animals have found a home in every type of environment on Earth.

MAMMAL MARKERS

Mammals are vertebrates. That means they have bony skeletons and backbones. They all share the following traits:

RACCOON p. 124

- They are **endothermic,** or warm-blooded. That means their body temperature stays mostly the same whether it's hot or cold outside.

- They have **hair.** Even smooth-skinned mammals such as whales are born with little hairs on their heads.

- Females feed their young with **milk.**

- They have **diaphragms,** muscles that separate the chest and the abdominal space that holds the stomach and other organs.

- They have some **unique bones** that other animals don't have, including three little bones in the middle ear.

TYPES OF MAMMALS

VIRGINIA OPOSSUM p. 16

There are three basic types of mammals, depending upon how their babies are born. A few, such as the Duck-billed Platypus, are monotremes. They give birth to babies in leathery eggs. Monotremes live only in Australia and New Guinea. Some mammals, such as the Virginia Opossum, are marsupials. Their babies are born only partly developed at birth. Then they climb into the mother's pouch to develop more. The rest, including humans, are placental mammals. They spend a long time inside

MOUNTAIN GOAT p. 142

the mother before they are born, and they are born live, not in eggs.

MAMMALS IN NORTH AMERICA

With landscapes ranging from mountains to deserts to swamps, there are many different kinds of mammals in North America—almost 500 species. They all have amazing ways of adapting to their surroundings. They can blend into the snow of the far North, build houses in eastern ponds, burrow under hot desert sand, and migrate thousands of miles to find the best places to eat and have their babies.

WHERE MAMMALS FIT IN

Biologists put all living things into groups that show how they are related. Each specific kind of animal has a scientific name in Latin. The first part of the name is its genus, which is its group of closely related animals. The second part of the scientific name is its species, which is special to that kind of animal only. For example, here is the classification for the Gray Wolf:

GRAY WOLF p. 107

Kingdom	Animalia (Animals)
Phylum	Chordata (Vertebrates)
Class	Mammalia (Mammals)
Order	Carnivora (Carnivores)
Family	Canidae (Dogs, Foxes, Wolves)
Genus	*Canis* (Dogs, Wolves, Coyotes)
Species	*Lupus*
Gray Wolf	*Canis lupus*

WHERE DID Mammals COME FROM?

HUNDREDS OF MILLIONS OF YEARS AGO, reptiles including massive dinosaurs ruled Earth. Then, more than 200 million years ago, little sharp-jawed reptiles called synapsids began to evolve into mammals. As dinosaurs became extinct around 65 million years ago, the environment changed and synapsids evolved more quickly, into many groups. In one group of these reptiles, their bodies became sleek and swift, with good hearing and the ability to chew a wide range of food. Instead of laying eggs, they began to give birth to live babies. They also began growing hair. Over millions of years these animals developed from reptiles into the wide range of mammals we see today.

ANCIENT BISON

GIANTS OF NORTH AMERICA

Prehistoric North America had plenty of small mammals, but until about 11,000 years ago it also had some giants that are now extinct. We're not sure why they died out. The first humans, coming onto the continent from Asia, may have hunted them into extinction. Or the giant mammals may have already been dying out because the climate was changing, and the biggest animals couldn't adapt. It is also possible that their extinctions were due to a combination of many things.

EARLY HUNTERS

Paleontologists—scientists who study dinosaurs and other ancient animals through fossil evidence—have pieced together what many of these animals looked like and how they lived. The continent had some amazing creatures, including the ones shown here.

MAMMOTHS

These big, hairy relatives of modern elephants were up to 13 feet (4 m) tall and weighed as much as 10 tons (9 t), about as much as a school bus. They probably lived in groups of females and their young, with males living alone.

GROUND SLOTHS

Unlike today's sloths, which live in trees, prehistoric ground sloths were huge, lumbering animals that lived on the ground. They were almost 10 feet (3 m) tall and weighed 2,200 pounds (1,000 kg). Standing up on their hind legs, they could grab leaves to eat using their long front legs and big claws.

GROUND SLOTH

CAMELS

Camels in North America? Yup! Ancient camels, of the genus *Camelops*, evolved on this continent and once roamed the American West. The biggest of these plant-eaters were a little larger than modern camels.

CAMELOPS

GIANT BEAVERS

Beavers today are hefty mammals, but they are tiny compared to North America's prehistoric giant beavers. Those rodents could be seven feet (2 m) long and weigh 276 pounds (125 kg), about the size of today's Black Bears. Like the beavers we see near ponds and streams, they had huge front teeth. The teeth of the ancient beavers were so big—up to six inches (15 cm) long—that they may have been too clumsy for chewing through wood.

GIANT BEAVER SKULL

GETTING STARTED: LOOKING FOR Mammals

NO MATTER WHERE YOU ARE IN NORTH AMERICA YOU CAN FIND MAMMALS. They climb in trees, tunnel through grass, burrow underground, and swim through rivers, lakes, and streams. They even swim in the ocean and fly through the air. Yet in a typical year we normally see only a few of the most common mammals, such as squirrels or Woodchucks. This is partly because most mammals come out only at night, or only at dawn and dusk. Most are also naturally shy of humans and will hide until we pass by. Even so, if you know where and how to look, you can spot mammals' paths, homes, and tracks as well as the creatures themselves. You just have to be patient and alert to the amazing mammals around you. Never feed wild animals or set food out to lure them—it's all about watching naturally!

WHITE-TAILED DEER p. 136

WHERE TO LOOK

Mammals often use paths near covered areas. Look for flattened pathways along or through hedges and shrubs, stone walls, and streams. Many animals travel through burrows and tunnels, so make sure you look down into the grass and under layers of leaves—and be careful not to disturb their passageways. Don't forget to look up as well. Some mammals nest in tree hollows and sleep on high tree limbs.

SEARCH AT DAWN OR DUSK

WHEN TO LOOK

Try getting up early or going out in the evening, when the light is dim. Then you may spot deer, rabbits, bats, raccoons, skunks, and other mammals that like the darker hours.

WHAT TO LOOK FOR

You can often find mammals by their signs. These include their tracks, which are easiest to see in wet places, such as along muddy paths or riverbanks. You'll see the tracks for all land mammals in the entries in this guide. Some animals like to claw trees or rub on rough tree bark, leaving scratch marks and tufts of fur behind. Squirrels and other rodents leave behind piles of nuts and shells in places where they sit to eat. And every animal poops. Left-behind animal dung, known as scat, can tell you if a deer, rabbit, or Moose has been by recently.

MUD TRACKS

DIRT TRACKS

TRACKING TIPS

When you go out mammal-watching, make sure you're prepared. Some dos and don'ts:

- ✓ **DO go with an adult or have an adult's permission.** Make sure that you're going someplace safe.

- ✓ **DON'T try to touch or pick up wild animals.** They will be frightened and may bite you.

- ✓ **DO wear soft clothes in layers,** including waterproof shoes if you'll be near streams or ponds. Make sure you tuck long pants into socks to protect against ticks.

- ✓ **DON'T wear anything with a strong smell.**

- ✓ **DO bring binoculars** for spotting animals high in trees or far away.

- ✓ **DO bring a small notebook and a pencil** so you can take notes on what you've seen and where you've seen it.

- ✓ **DON'T bring your dog.** You may love it, but other mammals do not.

- ✓ **DON'T touch animal scat (poop!);** it carries infection!

Virginia Opossum

Didelphis virginiana LENGTH 14–37 in (35.5–94 cm) • RANGE **Eastern and central U.S., West Coast (non-native)** • HABITAT **Forests and woods, fields, suburbs, cities** • FOOD **Fruit, nuts, insects, snakes, carrion** • ACTIVE ⓃⓁ

The Virginia Opossum is the United States' only marsupial—a mammal that carries its babies in a pouch. Opossums are cat-size creatures with stiff gray fur and white, pointy faces. Their noses are pink and their tails are long, naked, and prehensile (able to grab onto branches). These mammals are common in woods, fields, and backyards. They are usually seen at night, sometimes rooting about in garbage cans. Opossums are adaptable animals that live in other creatures' old burrows or dens. Once or twice a year, the female gives birth to up to 14 bean-size, naked babies. They crawl into her pouch and come out after about two months.

Be an ANIMAL ACE!

When faced with a hungry fox or nosy human, the Virginia Opossum doesn't run—it falls to the ground. Its mouth opens, it drools, and its eyes stare blankly. A predator that wants live food will go away. In a few minutes or a few hours, the opossum perks up and runs off to safety. People say the opossum is "playing dead," but there's no play about it. The response is automatic and out of the animal's control.

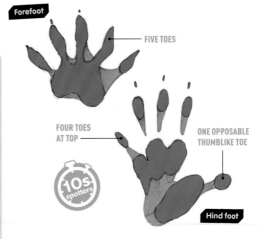

Forefoot

FIVE TOES

FOUR TOES AT TOP

ONE OPPOSABLE THUMBLIKE TOE

Hind foot

10s spotters

Nine-banded Armadillo

Dasypus novemcinctus **LENGTH 25–32 in
(63.5–81.5 cm)** • **RANGE Southeastern U.S., Texas to
Florida** • **HABITAT Fields, roadsides, areas with soft soil**
• **FOOD Insects, snails, worms, amphibians, bird eggs**
• **ACTIVE** 🅑 🌙

The Nine-banded Armadillo
looks like no other animal in
the United States. Bony skin
plates cover the top of its body
like a knight's coat of armor.
Nine flexible bands across its
back let it curl up and protect its
soft underside. This low-slung,
sturdy mammal has short legs, a slender head, and upright,
pointed ears. With poor eyesight but a good sense of smell, it
noses about in the dirt looking for food. The armadillo can
burrow to escape its enemies, but it's also surprisingly good
at crossing rivers. It will swallow air to float or walk across
the bottom without breathing for up to six minutes. Nine-
banded Armadillos have four identical babies once a year.

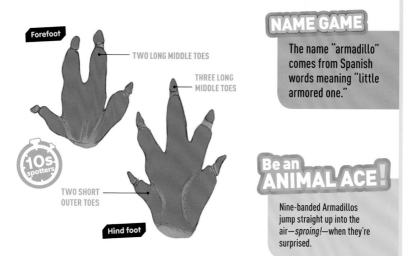

Forefoot

TWO LONG MIDDLE TOES

THREE LONG
MIDDLE TOES

10s
spotters

TWO SHORT
OUTER TOES

Hind foot

NAME GAME

The name "armadillo"
comes from Spanish
words meaning "little
armored one."

Be an ANIMAL ACE!

Nine-banded Armadillos
jump straight up into the
air—*sproing!*—when they're
surprised.

Mountain Beaver

Aplodontia rufa **LENGTH** 9–19 in (23–48.5 cm) • **RANGE** Pacific Northwest, Canada • **HABITAT** Wet forests, thick shrubs • **FOOD** Plants, including ferns, conifer twigs and needles • **ACTIVE** Ⓝ Ⓛ

FOREFOOT: SMALL, NARROW; FIVE TOES

HIND FOOT: LONGER THAN FOREFOOT; FIVE TOES

The Mountain Beaver is not a beaver at all, and it doesn't live in the mountains. It may have gotten this common name because it lives near water and chews on trees, like a beaver.

Mountain Beavers are shy rodents that live in long, narrow burrows in wooded areas. They are short and stocky with stubby little tails. Thick dark brown fur covers the tops of their bodies. Their undersides are paler brown. They are built for digging, with small ears and eyes and long front claws. They have one litter of three to five youngsters each year in spring.

NAME GAME

Another name for the Mountain Beaver is Sewellel (pronounced SUH-weh-lul). This may come from a Native American word for the animal's fur.

FOREFOOT: SMALL, TRIANGULAR; FOUR TOES

Abert's Squirrel

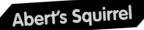

Sciurus aberti **LENGTH** 18–23 in (46–58.5 cm) • **RANGE** Arizona, New Mexico, Utah, Arizona • **HABITAT** Pine forests, other mixed forests • **FOOD** Plants, particularly pine nuts and twigs • **ACTIVE** Ⓓ Ⓛ

Abert's Squirrels love Ponderosa pine trees. They eat the trees' pine nuts and twigs and build nests high in the trees' branches. These large squirrels are active in the daytime. They have dark gray fur on their upper bodies and white fur on their undersides. One subspecies found only on the north rim of the Grand Canyon has an all-white tail. Their ears sport long, tufted tassels that are longer in winter and shorter in

HIND FOOT: LONG; FIVE TOES

summer. Females give birth to two to four babies in spring.

Eastern Gray Squirrel

Sciurus carolinensis LENGTH 15–20 in (38–51 cm) •
RANGE Eastern, central, and western (non-native) U.S., Canada
• HABITAT Woods, suburbs, cities • FOOD Nuts, seeds, buds,
fruit, insects, bird eggs • ACTIVE ☉ ☾

Scurrying down a tree, dashing
across a lawn, climbing up a bird
feeder: The Eastern Gray
Squirrel is the most commonly
seen mammal in the eastern
United States. This adaptable animal has short gray fur on the top of
its body and creamy fur on its belly.
Sometimes reddish fur is mixed in with
the gray. Eastern Gray Squirrels' big, bushy tails
have many uses: The squirrels flick them to say "hello," curl them
around their bodies for warmth, or hold them overhead as umbrellas
in the rain. Eastern Grays love to eat nuts, especially acorns. They
bury extra nuts one by one in the ground. In winter, they find them by
smell, even under a foot of snow. Look up into hardwood trees and
you will often see their leafy nests, though they also bed down in
holes inside trees. Twice a year, in spring and summer, females give
birth to two to four young.

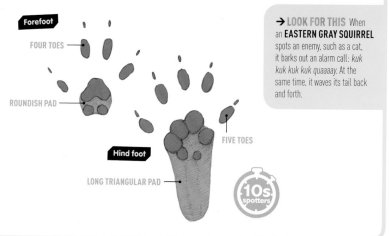

Forefoot

FOUR TOES

ROUNDISH PAD

Hind foot

FIVE TOES

LONG TRIANGULAR PAD

→ **LOOK FOR THIS** When
an **EASTERN GRAY SQUIRREL**
spots an enemy, such as a cat,
it barks out an alarm call: *kuk
kuk kuk kuk quaaaay.* At the
same time, it waves its tail back
and forth.

10s.
spotters

Western Gray Squirrel

Sciurus griseus LENGTH **18–23 in (46–58.5 cm)** ▪ RANGE **West Coast, Washington to California** ▪ HABITAT **Woods** ▪ FOOD **Acorns, pinecones, pine nuts, berries, insects** ▪ ACTIVE **D L**

Unlike their close relatives the Eastern Gray Squirrels, Western Gray Squirrels are shy and secretive animals. They are active during the day, but they like to stay hidden in the oak and pine trees that give them their favorite foods—acorns and pine nuts. Western Gray Squirrels have dark gray fur on their backs. Their gray, bushy tails have white edges; their bellies and the rings around their eyes are also white. Like other squirrels, including flying squirrels, they make their homes in holes in trees or in messy treetop nests of sticks and leaves called dreys. There they raise one litter of two to five youngsters each year.

EXPERT'S CIRCLE

DON'T BE FOOLED

Since some **Eastern Gray Squirrels** (page 19) now live in the West, it's easy to confuse them with their western cousins. You can tell Eastern Grays and Western Grays apart by size: Westerns are bigger. **Western Gray Squirrels** also have darker and grayer fur than Easterns; Easterns have more red mixed in.

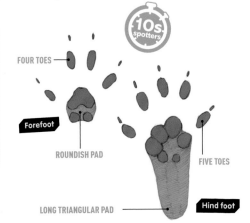

10s spotters

FOUR TOES

Forefoot

ROUNDISH PAD

FIVE TOES

LONG TRIANGULAR PAD

Hind foot

Eastern Fox Squirrel

Sciurus niger LENGTH 18–28 in (46–71 cm) • RANGE
Eastern and central U.S. • HABITAT Woods, suburbs •
FOOD Acorns, nuts, pinecones, berries • ACTIVE ☼ ☽

This large squirrel with a big, bushy
tail stays busy during the day finding, eating, or storing nuts. It has
gray or black fur on the top of its
body and rusty or yellowish fur on
its underside. Though it spends a
lot of time on the ground, the
Eastern Fox Squirrel lives in trees,
bunking down in holes or building
leafy nests in branches. Females have
two to four babies once or twice a year from spring to
summer. Eastern Fox Squirrels are becoming less common in the Southeast because the woods where they
make their homes are being cut down.

→ **LOOK FOR THIS** Have you
seen pieces of acorns or hickory
nutshells scattered on the ground
under a branch or stump? That's a
squirrel sign! **EASTERN FOX
SQUIRRELS** and others like to
perch in a favorite spot, snack
away on nuts, and drop the shells.

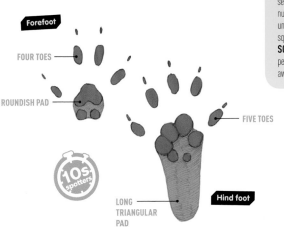

Forefoot

FOUR TOES

ROUNDISH PAD

FIVE TOES

10s spotters

LONG
TRIANGULAR
PAD

Hind foot

FOREFOOT: SMALL PAD; FOUR WIDELY SPACED TOES

Douglas's Squirrel

Tamiasciurus douglasii LENGTH 11–14 in (28–35.5 cm) ▪ RANGE Washington State through Northern California, Canada ▪ HABITAT Conifer forests ▪ FOOD Pinecones and pine twigs, acorns, nuts, mushrooms, berries ▪ ACTIVE 🌞 🌙

Small and noisy, this western squirrel is a bundle of energy. Naturalist John Muir called it "the wildest animal I ever saw,—a fiery, sputtering little bolt of life." Douglas's Squirrels have sleek, grayish brown fur on their backs. Their bellies are pale orange in summer. In winter, this color turns gray, and little tufts of fur appear on their ears. Douglas's Squirrels have a wide range of calls, from trills to barks to screams. Their four to six babies are born in late spring; sometimes they have another litter in the fall.

HIND FOOT: OVAL PAD; FIVE WIDELY SPACED TOES

NAME GAME

The Douglas's Squirrel is sometimes called the "Chickaree"—but so is the American Red Squirrel. John Muir wrote that Native Americans called it "Pillillooeet," after one of its calls. Try saying it superfast, emphasizing the first syllable: *PILL-illooeet*.

Red Squirrel

FOREFOOT: SMALL PAD; FOUR TOES

Tamiasciurus hudsonicus LENGTH 11–14 in (28–35.5 cm) ▪ RANGE Alaska, Rocky Mountains, Northeast into Appalachians, Canada ▪ HABITAT Conifer forests, mixed woods, hedges ▪ FOOD Pine nuts, acorns, nuts, mushrooms, berries, birds' eggs ▪ ACTIVE 🌞 🌙

Red squirrels don't like visitors. When another animal or a human gets too close, they will chatter and bark at them for up to an hour. These little squirrels have rusty red fur on their backs and sides and white bellies; in winter, they grow tufts of fur on their ears. Like many squirrels, Red Squirrels love the nuts that grow inside pinecones. They store pinecones in the ground and in holes in the trees and snack on them when they're hungry, leaving piles of pine scales behind. Females have three to seven babies in the spring, and sometimes another litter in late summer.

HIND FOOT: LARGER PAD; FIVE TOES

Southern Flying Squirrel

Glaucomys volans LENGTH 8–10 in (20.3–25.5 cm) • RANGE
Eastern half of U.S. • HABITAT Mixed woods, suburbs, cities •
FOOD Acorns, nuts, mushrooms, insects, birds • ACTIVE ◑ ◐

Southern Flying Squirrels don't
actually fly; instead they're
awesome gliders. Stretching
between their front and back
legs is thin skin covered with
silky fur. When this squirrel wants
to travel from tree to tree without
using the ground, it leaps into the
air and spreads its legs. The skin flat-
tens out like a kite, and the squirrel glides
for up to 262 feet (80 m) before landing on a tree
trunk. Southern Flying Squirrels are small, with big dark eyes.
They are gray on their upper sides, but their bellies are white.
Flattened tails help them glide. Although these squirrels are
common in the eastern United States, you won't see them
often. Unlike many tree squirrels, they are active at night and
sleep in tree holes during the day. In spring and sometimes
again in late summer, they have two to seven babies.

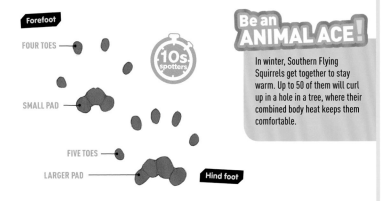

Forefoot

FOUR TOES

SMALL PAD

FIVE TOES

LARGER PAD

Hind foot

10s. spotters

Be an ANIMAL ACE!

In winter, Southern Flying
Squirrels get together to stay
warm. Up to 50 of them will curl
up in a hole in a tree, where their
combined body heat keeps them
comfortable.

Northern Flying Squirrel

Glaucomys sabrinus **LENGTH 10–14 in (25.5–35.5 cm)**
- **RANGE Northern U.S, eastern and western mountains, Canada**
- **HABITAT Conifer forests, mixed woods** • **FOOD Mushrooms, lichens, nuts, birds, eggs** • **ACTIVE N L**

Like its relative the Southern Flying Squirrel, the Northern Flying Squirrel is a master glider. The furry membrane between its outstretched legs, plus its flat tail, lets it sail from tree to tree. These small rodents have large dark eyes, brown fur on their upper bodies, and white fur with gray roots on their bellies. They are active at night. Even if you can't see them, you might hear their soft, birdlike chirps in the dark. Northern Flying Squirrels build nests in tree holes, such as those left in tall dead stumps by woodpeckers. Females have two to five babies once a year in the spring.

EXPERT'S CIRCLE

DON'T BE FOOLED

Both **Northern** and **Southern Flying Squirrels** (page 23) live in the Northeast. You can tell them apart by size—Northerns are a little bigger—and by color. Northern fliers have brown upper fur and their belly fur is gray at the roots. Southern Flying Squirrels have gray upper fur and pure white bellies.

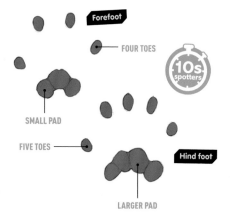

Forefoot

FOUR TOES

SMALL PAD

FIVE TOES

Hind foot

LARGER PAD

10s. spotters

Harris's Antelope Squirrel

Ammospermophilus harrisii LENGTH 9–10 in (23–25.5 cm) • RANGE Arizona, southwestern New Mexico • HABITAT Deserts • FOOD Cactus and yucca seeds, fruit, mesquite beans, insects • ACTIVE ⬤ ⬤

Burning heat and spiny plants don't bother the Harris's Antelope Squirrel. This ground squirrel, native to southwestern deserts, will run about in the daytime looking for seeds and beans to eat. Sometimes it climbs to the top of a prickly cholla cactus to look around. To keep cool, it holds its gray tail over its back like an umbrella against the sun. It will also practice "heat dumping": spreading out flat in a shady spot so its body heat soaks into the ground. Similar to chipmunks, they have grayish brown upper bodies, white bellies, and a white stripe up each side. They live in burrows near shrubs or trees where they have one litter of four to nine babies each winter.

FOREFOOT: SMALL PAD; FOUR TOES

HIND FOOT: SLIGHTLY LARGER PAD; FIVE TOES

EXPERT'S CIRCLE

DON'T BE FOOLED

Harris's and **White-tailed Antelope Squirrels** (below) look much alike. Where their ranges overlap, you can tell them apart by their tails. The Harris's' tail is black and white on the underside, while the White-tailed's tail is pure white on the bottom.

White-tailed Antelope Squirrel

Ammospermophilus leucurus LENGTH 8–9 in (20.3–23 cm) • RANGE Southern Oregon and Idaho to Southern California, northern Arizona, and northwestern New Mexico • HABITAT Deserts, dry rocky areas • FOOD Green plants, seeds, insects • ACTIVE ⬤ ⬤

FOREFOOT: SMALL PAD; FOUR TOES

White-tailed Antelope Squirrels are tough little creatures that can survive in hot southwestern summers and chilly northwestern winters. When the weather is too hot, they rest in their shady burrows. When it's cold, they huddle together underground. These ground squirrels are grayish or tan on their upper bodies and white below. Their tails, often held flat over their backs, are white on the underside. A white stripe marks each side of their bodies. In spring, White-tailed Antelope Squirrels have one litter of 5 to 14 babies.

HIND FOOT: SLIGHTLY LARGER PAD; FIVE TOES

White-tailed Prairie Dog

Cynomys leucurus LENGTH 13–15 in (33–38 cm) • RANGE Southern Montana to northern Colorado • HABITAT Mountain meadows and pastures • FOOD Green plants, shrubs • ACTIVE ◐ ◖

HIND FOOT: FIVE LONG TOES; LARGER PAD

FOREFOOT: FOUR LONG TOES; SMALL PAD

It may have "prairie" in its name, but the White-tailed Prairie Dog is a mountain animal. In high meadows and pastures in the West, it makes its home in burrows marked by mounds at the entrance. These stocky mammals have tan to gray fur on their backs and paler undersides; their short tails have white tips. They are not as sociable as their Black-tailed relatives. Living in small colonies, they search for grasses and shrubs to eat during the summer while keeping an eye out for enemies: Coyotes, Bobcats, badgers, hawks, eagles, and humans—who kill them as pests. In the cold mountain winters, these prairie dogs hibernate until March or so. They have one litter of four to six pups in the spring.

Hoary Marmot

Marmota caligata LENGTH 18–32 in (46–81.5 cm) • RANGE Alaska into Washington, Idaho, Montana, Canada • HABITAT Mountain meadows and rocky slopes • FOOD Green plants and grasses • ACTIVE ◑ ◖

HIND FOOT: LARGE PAD; FIVE TOES

That loud whistling alarm call you hear in a western mountain meadow may come from a Hoary Marmot, whose nickname is "Whistler." Hoary Marmots are stocky rodents the size of small dogs. "Hoary" means gray or white, like an old person's hair, and the Hoary Marmot does have grizzled gray hair on the front half of its body. Its back half is a warm reddish brown. White patches of fur mark its nose and forehead. Because they live in cold, high places, Hoary Marmots hibernate during the winter. Every other spring, females give birth to two to four babies. The families stay together for a couple of years, living in big underground burrows and finding food in summer.

FOREFOOT: FRONT AND BACK PAD; FOUR TOES

NAME GAME

The Hoary Marmot's species name, *caligata*, means "booted." Hoary Marmots have dark brown or black feet, like boots.

Black-tailed Prairie Dog

Cynomys ludovicianus LENGTH 14–16 in (35.5–40.5 cm) •
RANGE Montana to Texas • HABITAT Shortgrass prairies • FOOD Green
plants, insects • ACTIVE 🌞 🌙

"Yip! Yip!" That jumping, yipping
Black-tailed Prairie Dog is telling its
neighbors that all is clear—no enemies are in sight. Neighbors are
important to prairie dogs. They are
sociable animals that live in underground "towns" made of tunnels that can
stretch for hundreds of acres. Each town is
divided into neighborhoods with "coteries"—
family groups with one male, several females, and
youngsters. The entrances to the tunnels are marked with mounds,
where the prairie dogs look around for danger. With orangish brown fur
above and pale fur below, these prairie dogs have small tails tipped with
black fur. Once a year, in spring, females give birth to three or four
babies. Black-tailed Prairie Dogs once ruled the grasslands, but because
it was believed that they ate so much grass and built mounds that could
trip horses, ranchers killed off many of them. They still live throughout
the prairies, but in much smaller numbers than in the past.

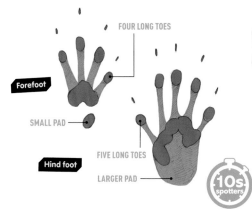

FOUR LONG TOES

Forefoot

SMALL PAD

FIVE LONG TOES

Hind foot

LARGER PAD

10s
spotters

Be an ANIMAL ACE!

The biggest prairie dog towns
used to be the size of human
cities. One Texas town spread out
underground for 25,000 square
miles (64,750 sq km) and may
have held 400 million prairie dogs.

Woodchuck

Marmota monax LENGTH 17–32 in (43–81.5 cm) • RANGE Alaska east into central and northeastern U.S., Canada • HABITAT Fields, woods, roadsides • FOOD Green plants, crops • ACTIVE 🌙 🌘

Also known as Groundhogs, Woodchucks are common sights along grassy roadsides. These low-slung rodents enjoy being out in the sun scouting for tasty plants to eat. When danger threatens, they scurry back to their burrows, where they live year-round. Woodchucks have grizzled grayish or brownish fur, bushy tails, and short ears. They are surprisingly athletic. Woodchucks can swim well, climb trees, and dig a burrow in minutes flat. In winter, they go into a deep hibernation. Their body temperatures drop to 35°F (1.6°C) and their heartbeats slow to four beats a minute. In spring, they wake up and come out to find mates. Females give birth to one to seven youngsters each year.

Be an ANIMAL ACE!

Marmota monax may be the only mammal with its own holiday: Groundhog Day! Each February 2, officials in Punxsutawney, Pennsylvania, pull Punxsutawney Phil out of a burrow to see if he casts a shadow. Supposedly, a shadow means six more weeks of winter. However, Phil and his shadow can't really predict the weather. The most they can predict is that Phil is probably one grumpy Groundhog every February 2.

Forefoot

FOUR TOES

FIVE TOES

10s spotters

FRONT AND BACK PADS

Hind foot

LARGE PAD

Yellow-bellied Marmot

Marmota flaviventris **LENGTH 19–28 in (48.5–71 cm)**
• **RANGE Western U.S. into New Mexico, Canada** • **HABITAT Mountain meadows in rocky areas** • **FOOD Green plants**
• **ACTIVE** 🌣 🌙

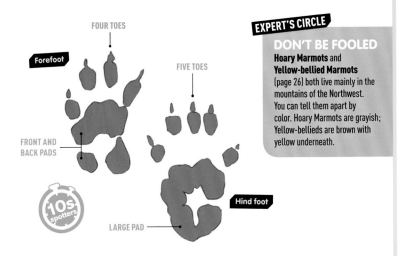

Although the Yellow-bellied Marmot has adapted to different habitats, it is especially at home in high places. It digs its burrows into high, rocky, mountain slopes. There, it can perch on a rock to watch for danger or snack on green plants. If it spots an enemy, it whistles, screams, or chatters its teeth. These marmots are stocky, with thick brownish fur on their backs, yellow fur on their bellies, and bushy tails. They eat as much as they can all summer so that by the fall they're pretty fat. This is healthy, for a marmot. Their bodies use up that fat as fuel all winter while they hibernate. In spring, they come out of hibernation and have one litter of about five young.

FOUR TOES

Forefoot

FIVE TOES

FRONT AND BACK PADS

10s. spotters

LARGE PAD

Hind foot

EXPERT'S CIRCLE

DON'T BE FOOLED

Hoary Marmots and **Yellow-bellied Marmots** (page 26) both live mainly in the mountains of the Northwest. You can tell them apart by color. Hoary Marmots are grayish; Yellow-bellieds are brown with yellow underneath.

MAMMAL MANIA: CLOSED FOR THE WINTER

LITTLE BROWN MYOTIS BATS HIBERNATE IN WINTER.

Mammals need energy to stay warm. To make that energy, they have to eat plenty of food. But in winter, food is scarce and the weather can be deadly. So some cold-climate mammals hibernate—enter a sleeplike state—in winter. Their body temperatures drop. Their hearts slow down. They may breathe only a few times a minute. They live off the body fat that they stored during warmer months. Some go into deep hibernation. They are cold and still and barely move for months. Others, like bears, move in and out of a state called torpor; their body temperature drops to conserve energy, and they sleep for shorter periods.

Deep Sleepers

Arctic Ground Squirrels (page 33) are world-class hibernators. From September through April, they curl up in their burrows. Their heart rates drop to about one beat per minute. Their body temperatures sink below freezing. They lose almost half of their body fat before they wake in spring.

Bear-ly Moving

For an American Black Bear (page 110), how much it sleeps during the winter depends on where it lives. In warm places, only pregnant females sleep much of the time. In cold areas, all American Black Bears sleep away the winter. They don't go into deep hibernation, but into a state called torpor: Their body temperatures drop a few degrees and their heart rates drop from a normal resting rate of 66 beats per minute (bpm) to 8 to 22 bpm. However, they don't eat, drink, or even pee until spring.

Comfort in Crowds

When bats hibernate, they do it together. In the fall, bats called Little Brown Myotis (page 99) fly hundreds of miles to particular caves or unused mines to hibernate by the thousands. These kinds of hibernation spaces are called hibernacula. The bats wake up every few weeks, and move around to keep their bodies healthy, but they don't eat. By spring, they have lost most of their body fat.

Columbian Ground Squirrel

Urocitellus columbianus LENGTH 13–16 in (33–40.5 cm)
• RANGE Oregon, Idaho, Montana, Canada • HABITAT Mountain meadows,
fields • FOOD Green plants, seeds, insects, birds • ACTIVE 🌑 🌙

Columbian Ground Squirrels pack a lot of action into about 100 days during the spring and summer. The rest of the time, they hibernate in their burrows. These sturdy rodents live in chilly regions of the Northwest. Their fur, grizzled gray and brown on their backs, is a warm brown on their faces, legs, and bellies. Their tails are bushy and reddish. Though they live in colonies, they are very territorial: Each Columbian Ground Squirrel will defend its home area and drive away other squirrels. In warm weather, they are busy putting on weight and watching out for predators. In late summer, they begin their hibernation in underground dens. These dens are cozy! Lined with grass, they have drains to let water run out, plugs of earth to block them from the outside, and stores of food. In late spring, first males, and then females, come out. They give birth to a litter of three to five young each year.

→ **LOOK FOR THIS** Are those ground squirrels kissing? Kind of. **COLUMBIAN GROUND SQUIRRELS** and some other members of the squirrel family greet each other by sniffing and touching each other, mouth to mouth. This behavior might help strengthen social ties.

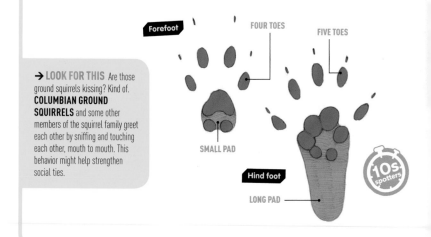

Forefoot

FOUR TOES

FIVE TOES

SMALL PAD

Hind foot

LONG PAD

10S. spotters

Arctic Ground Squirrel

Urocitellus parryii LENGTH 12–16 in (30.5–40.5 cm) ▪ RANGE Alaska, Canada ▪ HABITAT Meadows, tundra, hills ▪ FOOD Green plants, seeds, berries, insects, dead animals ▪ ACTIVE ☀ ☾

FOREFOOT: SMALL PAD; FOUR TOES

HIND FOOT: LONG PAD; FIVE TOES

Tough little critters, Arctic Ground Squirrels live in far northern regions where winters are long and harsh. They are fairly large ground squirrels, with grizzled orange/grayish/brownish fur on their backs and paler, yellowish underparts. They make their homes in winding burrows, which can be dug only where the ground has thawed out at least three feet (0.9 m) below the surface. In the burrows, they build snug nesting dens lined with grasses or soft caribou fur. For more than six months, they hibernate in these dens. Males come out first, sometimes digging through snow in temperatures that are still below freezing. In summer, females give birth to 5 to 10 young. The young grow fast during the short, warm months, taking in the sun while they can before they retreat underground for another winter.

FOREFOOT: SMALL PAD; FOUR TOES

Franklin's Ground Squirrel

Poliocitellus franklinii LENGTH 15–16 in (38–40.5 cm) ▪ RANGE North-central U.S., Canada ▪ HABITAT Grassy and brushy areas ▪ FOOD Green plants, seeds, insects, eggs, small animals ▪ ACTIVE ☀ ☾

HIND FOOT: LONG PAD; FIVE TOES

You might not expect it from a squirrel, but the Franklin's Ground Squirrel is quite a meat-eater. These northern rodents eat plants, but they also enjoy munching on birds, toads, and small hares. Like many ground squirrels, they're fattening up for a long winter's hibernation. Franklin's Ground Squirrels have grizzled gray-brown fur on their backs, pale fur on their bellies, small ears, and narrow bushy tails. They're out in the daytime, but they can be hard to see. They live in tall grasses and will scoot for their burrows at the first sign of danger. Even if you can't see them, you might hear their loud, trilling alarm whistles. After hibernating up to eight months, they emerge in spring and give birth to five to eight youngsters.

California Ground Squirrel

Otospermophilus beecheyi LENGTH 14–20 in (35.5–51 cm) ▪ RANGE
Southern Washington and western Oregon through California ▪ HABITAT
Fields, croplands, open areas ▪ FOOD Green plants, seeds, flowers, fruit,
insects, birds ▪ ACTIVE ☀ ☾

California Ground Squirrels like farms, but farmers don't like them. The busy western rodents enjoy eating grains and fruits from planted crops. When they can't get those, they'll eat anything from insects crawling on the ground to garbage from trash cans. They are fairly large ground squirrels, with grizzled brownish fur on their backs and creamy underparts. Whitish hair covers their neck and shoulders around a V-shaped patch of darker fur. Like other ground squirrels, they live in burrows, although they are not very sociable. In winter, they hibernate. One litter of three to nine young is born each year around May.

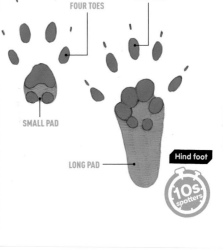

Forefoot

FOUR TOES

FIVE TOES

SMALL PAD

LONG PAD

Hind foot

10s spotters

DANGER! ☠

You know this, but it's worth repeating: Don't touch wild animals! Not only can frightened animals hurt you or themselves, but some also carry insects that spread diseases. California Ground Squirrels, as well as some other rodents, can carry the fleas that spread bubonic plague. Stay clear and stay safe.

Rock Squirrel

Otospermophilus variegatus **LENGTH 17–21 in (43–53.5 cm) • RANGE Southwestern U.S. • HABITAT Cliffs, canyons, other rocky areas • FOOD Nuts, seeds, fruit, green plants, small animals • ACTIVE D L**

FOREFOOT: SMALL PAD; FOUR TOES
10s spotters
HIND FOOT: LONG PAD; FIVE TOES

This big ground squirrel with a bushy tail looks a lot like a tree squirrel. Sometimes it even climbs trees in search of fruit and nuts. Most of the time, though, it lives on and under rocks in family burrows. Usually, a female defends her family burrow against outsiders, while the main male squirrel drives away other males. The Rock Squirrel has grizzled brown fur with a spotted or wavy pattern on its back and a creamy underside. Living as it does in warm places, it may be active outdoors all year. In the coldest parts of its range, it hibernates briefly. In spring and summer, females give birth to two litters of three to nine young each.

Be an ANIMAL ACE!

In nature, the rule is "waste not, want not." That applies to ground squirrel burrows. When ground squirrels move out of their burrows, other animals often move in—creatures such as burrowing owls or foxes.

Spotted Ground Squirrel

Xerospermophilus spilosoma **LENGTH 7–10 in (17.8–25.5 cm) • RANGE South Dakota and eastern Wyoming to southwestern U.S. • HABITAT Dry, sandy or grassy areas • FOOD Grasses, seeds, insects • ACTIVE D L**

FOREFOOT: SMALL PAD; FOUR TOES
10s spotters
HIND FOOT: LONG PAD; FIVE TOES

If you want to spot the Spotted Ground Squirrel, try mornings and evenings, when the weather is cooler. At those times, the little mammals come out of their burrows to look for grass, seeds, or insects to eat. Spotted Ground Squirrels are small—about half the size of most other ground squirrels—with pale spots dotting the gray or brown fur on their backs. Their tails are skinny with dark tips. In the northern parts of their range, they hibernate in winter. In spring and again in summer, they give birth to a litter of five to seven youngsters.

Thirteen-lined Ground Squirrel

Ictidomys tridecemlineatus LENGTH 7–12 in (17.8–30.5 cm)
• RANGE Central U.S., Canada • HABITAT Grassy areas, roadsides,
golf courses • FOOD Grasses, seeds, insects, small animals
• ACTIVE 🌞 🌙

The Thirteen-lined Ground Squirrel does in fact have 13 lines. These pale and dark lines run down its back and sides. Inside the dark lines are tidy rows of pale spots. The squirrels' cheeks and undersides are pale and their tails are slender. The only ground squirrel species in the central United States, these little mammals build shallow burrows in grassy areas. They especially like mowed places, like yards or golf courses, where you might see them standing up to look around. In winter, Thirteen-lined Ground Squirrels go into deep hibernation. They roll into a ball, their body temperature drops, and they breathe only four times a minute. In spring, they give birth to one litter of 6 to 13 babies.

NAME GAME

Many people in the Midwest know Thirteen-lined Ground Squirrels as "gophers"—and in summer there are plenty of complaints about stepping in a gopher hole in the backyard. The University of Minnesota Golden Gopher mascot is actually one of these ground squirrels.

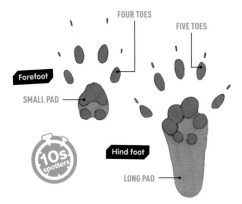

FOUR TOES

FIVE TOES

Forefoot

SMALL PAD

Hind foot

LONG PAD

10s spotters

Golden-mantled Ground Squirrel

Callospermophilus lateralis LENGTH 9–12 in (23–30.5 cm) ▪ RANGE
Western U.S., Canada ▪ HABITAT Mountain meadows, forests, brushy and rocky areas
▪ FOOD Fungi, seeds, nuts, green plants, insects, small animals ▪ ACTIVE 🅓 🅛

Golden-mantled Ground Squirrels are familiar
sights at western campgrounds, where they beg
openly for food. They are colorful little creatures.
Their heads and shoulders are a warm orange-red;
thick black and white stripes run up each side. Their
bellies are pale and tails are slender. Each one lives in
its own shallow burrow, which typically opens up at the bottom of a log
or rock. Like most northern ground squirrels, Golden-mantled Ground
Squirrels fatten up during the summer and hibernate through the winter. In early summer, the females have one litter of four to six young.

FOREFOOT:
SMALL PAD;
FOUR TOES

HIND FOOT:
LONG PAD;
FIVE TOES

FOREFOOT:
SMALL PAD;
FOUR LONG SLENDER TOES

Alpine Chipmunk

Tamias alpinus LENGTH 7–8 in (17.8–20.3 cm) ▪ RANGE Sierra Nevada mountains of
California ▪ HABITAT Mountain meadows, forests, and rocky slopes ▪ FOOD Seeds, fungi,
berries ▪ ACTIVE 🅓 🅛

Little and lively, Alpine Chipmunks live high
in the rocky Sierra Nevada mountains in
California. You might spot them dashing
about mountain slopes or pulling on grass
stalks to stuff grass seeds into their big
cheeks. Their pale grayish fur is decorated
with brown and white stripes down their backs
and across the sides of their heads. Orange fur
covers their sides and bellies. Alpine Chipmunks
hibernate through the long winters, emerging in
early summer to give birth to four or five young.

HIND FOOT:
LARGER PAD;
FIVE LONG SLENDER TOES

EXPERT'S CIRCLE

DON'T BE FOOLED What's the difference between **ground squirrels** (opposite and top) and
chipmunks (above)? Not much! They're all squirrels that live on and under the ground. However, chipmunks
belong to a single genus, *Tamias*. They are typically smaller than ground squirrels and their stripes extend
across their heads. And they all have "chipmunk cheeks": furry pouches that can hold lots of seeds and nuts.

Eastern Chipmunk

Tamias striatus LENGTH **9–12 in (23–30.5 cm)** • RANGE **Eastern half of U.S., Canada** • HABITAT **Open woods, woodland edges, yards, gardens** • FOOD **Nuts, seeds, berries, fungi, insects** • ACTIVE **D** **L**

The Eastern Chipmunk is a common sight in many yards and parks. These little rodents are a warm reddish brown on top with a dark stripe down their backs and dark-edged white stripes down their sides. Pale stripes sweep past their eyes. Eastern Chipmunks love nuts, such as acorns, and can pack hundreds of them into their underground nests to snack on in winter. They can be noisy, piping up with a high *chip* that sounds like a bird chirping. In winter, they hibernate, although some will wake up once in a while to venture outside. In spring, females have one litter of three to five young.

TRY THIS!

You, too, can be a mammal scientist. The best way is to find a good viewing place—maybe a window, or a bench at a local park. Pick a squirrel or other mammal you often see in daytime and take notes in all seasons. Each time, write down:

• The date
• The time of day
• The place (where in the yard or park)
• What it's doing
• What it eats
• What sounds it makes

You can even make sketches to help you identify different species. Soon you'll realize you've learned a lot!

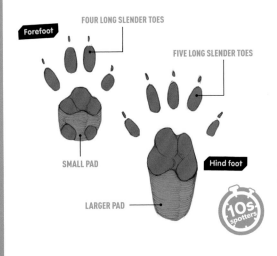

Forefoot

FOUR LONG SLENDER TOES

FIVE LONG SLENDER TOES

SMALL PAD

Hind foot

LARGER PAD

10S-spotters

Cliff Chipmunk

Tamias dorsalis **LENGTH** 8–11 in (20.3–28 cm) • **RANGE** Southwestern U.S. • **HABITAT** Canyons and cliffs with mixed forests • **FOOD** Seeds, nuts, berries, insects, small animals • **ACTIVE** 🇩 🇱

Cliff Chipmunks are at home in the rocks. They run up canyon walls with ease and store food and make their dens under boulders. Blending into the rocks, their backs are a smoky gray. Dull stripes run down their sides, where the fur turns orange and then white on the belly. Brighter stripes mark their pointed heads. Cliff Chipmunks keep watch for many enemies, such as Coyotes and hawks. When they see danger, they may freeze in place, bark or chirp, and twitch their tails. After a winter's hibernation, the females give birth to one litter of about four to five young in the summer.

FOREFOOT: SMALL PAD; FOUR LONG SLENDER TOES

HIND FOOT: LARGER PAD; FIVE LONG SLENDER TOES

Laugh Out Loud!

Why did the other animals avoid the chipmunk?

Because he drove them nuts!

FOREFOOT: SMALL PAD; FOUR LONG SLENDER TOES

Merriam's Chipmunk

Tamias merriami **LENGTH** 8–11 in (20.3–28 cm) • **RANGE** Central and Southern California • **HABITAT** Dry shrubby areas, mixed woods, high rocky areas • **FOOD** Seeds, nuts, insects, birds, eggs • **ACTIVE** 🇩 🇱

Merriam's Chipmunks often copy their relatives, the tree squirrels: They like to climb trees and leap from branch to branch. Some even nest in trees, making dens in stumps and hollow trunks. Grayish brown to reddish with dark stripes on top, Merriam's Chipmunks have white bellies and long bushy tails. These tails may help them balance as they jump about. Unlike many chipmunks, they don't hibernate. Females attract mates in spring by perching on high places and calling *chip chip chip* for hours. Their babies are born in late spring or summer, in litters of about three to six babies.

HIND FOOT: LARGER PAD; FIVE LONG SLENDER TOES

FOREFOOT:
SMALL PAD;
FOUR LONG SLENDER TOES

HIND FOOT:
LARGER PAD;
FIVE LONG SLENDER TOES

Least Chipmunk

Tamias minimus LENGTH 7–9 in (17.8–23 cm) ◦ RANGE Western U.S. and upper Midwest, Canada ◦ HABITAT Pine forests, mountain meadows, cliffs, deserts ◦ FOOD Acorns, seeds, fruits, grasses ◦ ACTIVE 🌞 🌙

It's called the "Least" Chipmunk because of its small size, but it's not the least common chipmunk. In fact, Least Chipmunks are widespread. They're found throughout the West, from mountains to deserts, as well as in the upper Midwest around the Great Lakes. These little mammals come in a wide variety of colors across their range. In drier places, they have pale yellowish gray fur with tan stripes. In wetter areas, their fur is darker, a brownish gray with black stripes on the side. The underside of their long bushy tails may be yellowish, reddish, or brown. These adaptable animals sleep and hibernate in burrows and rocky dens. In the winter, they may wake at times to snack on the seeds they've stored underground. In spring, the chipmunks come out and the females give birth to three to six tiny young.

Townsend's Chipmunk

FOREFOOT:
SMALL PAD;
FOUR LONG SLENDER TOES

Tamias townsendii LENGTH 9–14 in (23–35.5 cm) ◦ RANGE Oregon and Washington, Canada ◦ HABITAT Damp forests and clear-cut areas with fallen logs ◦ FOOD Nuts, fungi, berries, seeds ◦ ACTIVE 🌞 🌙

Townsend's Chipmunks are natives of the Pacific Northwest. There, they scamper about in moist forests and collect mushrooms and seeds to eat. They are larger and darker than most chipmunks, with brown fur and wide dark and pale stripes across their heads and backs. Their tails are long, bushy, and dark on top. Named for 19th-century adventurer John Kirk Townsend, who first described them, they run up trees to escape predators like mink and weasels. In colder areas, they hibernate through the winter. Females have litters of two to six youngsters.

HIND FOOT:
LARGER PAD;
FIVE LONG SLENDER TOES

American Beaver

Castor canadensis **LENGTH** 3–4 ft (0.9–1.2 m) •
RANGE Canada, most of U.S. except Florida, Nevada, and
Southern California • **HABITAT** Rivers, streams, ponds,
lakes, swamps • **FOOD** Bark, twigs, leaves • **ACTIVE** Ⓝ Ⓛ

Most animals adapt to their surroundings. Not the American Beaver! It changes its surroundings to suit itself. This remarkable animal, the largest North American rodent, is a master builder. It uses its big orange incisors—its front teeth—to chop down small trees. Then it carries the wood into streams and ponds to build dams, as well as homes called lodges. Some river beavers, known as bank beavers, just live in a hole in a riverbank. Beavers are big, heavy, and well adapted to a watery life. They have thick, shiny brown fur and webbed feet. Their tails are broad and flat, good for steering while swimming and for slapping the water loudly when danger is spotted. Though American Beavers are nighttime animals, you may see them in the evening and at other times of the day. They mate for life, giving birth to four or five babies, called kits, in late spring.

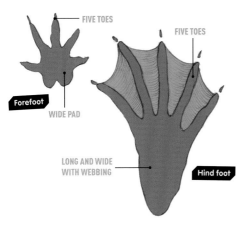

FIVE TOES

FIVE TOES

Forefoot

WIDE PAD

LONG AND WIDE
WITH WEBBING

Hind foot

Be an ANIMAL ACE!

Beaver lodges are amazing structures. Beavers build them out of slender trees such as willows or poplars, which they can chew down in just a few minutes. Then they trim off the branches and carry them into the water. The lodge rises up out of the still water in a mound. Entrances are underwater, and the upper area has two dry rooms. Beavers plaster the outside with mud, which hardens to form a strong shell.

MAMMAL MANIA: PLAYING DEFENSE

A SNOWSHOE HARE "HIDES" BY BLENDING IN WITH ITS WINTRY SURROUNDINGS.

Most mammals live in constant danger from predators. They wouldn't survive for long without good defenses. Some have colors that hide them in the grass or trees. Many live in groups with a lookout that calls out a warning when an enemy comes near. Some are simply too big to eat or too fast to be caught. And a few, such as the ones shown here, have developed amazing bodies and behaviors to defend themselves.

Armor-dillo

The Nine-banded Armadillo (page 17) is literally a tough animal. Its head, back, sides, and tail are covered by scutes—bony, scaly plates. In between the rows of scutes is softer skin, which allows armadillos to bend. Their undersides and inner legs don't have armor, but they do have thick skin and hair. Unlike their South American cousins, these armadillos do not roll up into a ball to protect themselves. When attacked, armadillos will run, dig a trench, and then show only their hard, armored backs and tails to predators.

A Prickly Problem

Very few predators will attack the North American Porcupine (page 44). Mixed into its thick hair are 30,000 sharp quills. A quill is actually a kind of hair, stiff and sharp and covered with tiny barbed scales. When a porcupine slaps its tail into an enemy, the barbs slide into the enemy and are hard to pull out. Meanwhile, the porcupine escapes and in time grows new quills to replace the old ones.

Stink Bomb

Skunks (pages 120–122) don't have to be fast or strong to survive. They just have to be stinky. Skunks have two glands on their rears that are filled with an oily, very smelly liquid that contains sulfur chemicals. When threatened, skunks turn, raise their tails, and spray their enemies. They can hit a target from 12 feet (3.5 m) away. While the attacker is pawing its eyes and backing off, the skunk strolls away.

North American Porcupine

Erethizon dorsatum LENGTH **26–37 in (66–94 cm)** ▪ RANGE **Alaska, western U.S., Great Lakes, Northeast, Canada** ▪ HABITAT **Mixed forests, scrublands in West** ▪ FOOD **Bark, inner wood of trees, leaves, twigs, nuts** ▪ ACTIVE 🌑 🌓

**FOREFOOT:
FLAT PRINT WITH
PEBBLY MARKINGS;
FOUR TOES**

The good news: If you don't mess with a North American Porcupine, it won't mess with you. This big, slow-moving rodent is famous for the sharp quills on its back and tail. Long brown guard hairs cover the front half of its short-legged body. When threatened, the porcupine turns around and raises its tail, quills rising up. If the enemy keeps coming, the tail lashes out, driving the quills into the enemy's skin. When it's not threatened, the porcupine is a peaceful mammal. It loves to eat bark and the soft wood underneath bark. Using its sharp claws and tail quills, it's a good tree climber. Porcupines live in holes, hollow trees, or logs. They give birth to one baby in early summer.

....

**FOREFOOT:
SMALL ROUNDED PRINT;
FOUR TOES**

Banner-tailed Kangaroo Rat

Dipodomys spectabilis LENGTH **12–15 in (30.5–38 cm)** ▪ RANGE **Texas, New Mexico, Arizona** ▪ HABITAT **Dry grassy or sandy plains, shrubs, gravelly areas** ▪ FOOD **Seeds, green plants** ▪ ACTIVE 🌑

Using its long, strong hind feet, the Banner-tailed Kangaroo Rat can leap almost nine feet (2.7 m) through the air. This native of the dry Southwest has yellow-tan sides marked with white stripes that run partway down the tail. Its undersides are white. The long tail has a bright white tip that seems to fly through the air like a banner when the animal runs. During the day, these mammals escape the desert heat in mounded burrows.

**HIND FOOT:
NARROW PRINT;
FOUR TOES**

There they give birth to one to three litters of two to three youngsters each year. Because their habitat is changing, these rodents are becoming less common and they are considered near threatened.

Ord's Kangaroo Rat

Dipodomys ordii LENGTH 8–11 in (20.3–28 cm) ▪ RANGE Western U.S., Canada ▪ HABITAT Dry grasslands, scrub, sand dunes ▪ FOOD Seeds, green plants ▪ ACTIVE **N** **L**

This hopper seems to be all head and feet. The Ord's Kangaroo Rat has long hind legs, short front legs, and a short, sleek body. Its fur is brownish or reddish on top and white below. A dark stripe runs down its tail. It lives in burrows throughout the dry Southwest and collects seeds to store underground. Like other kangaroo rats, it will drum its long feet on the ground when danger approaches. The brave little rodent also uses those feet to kick sand at enemies, such as rattlesnakes. Once or twice a year, it has a litter of one to six youngsters.

FOREFOOT: SMALL ROUNDED PRINT; FOUR TOES

HIND FOOT: NARROW PRINT; FOUR TOES

HIND FOOT: LONG SKINNY PRINT; FIVE TOES

California Pocket Mouse

Chaetodipus californicus LENGTH 7–9 in (17.8–23 cm) ▪ RANGE Central and Southern California ▪ HABITAT Grasslands, woods, scrubby areas ▪ FOOD Seeds, plants, insects ▪ ACTIVE **N** **L**

At night, California Pocket Mice come out of their burrows to find seeds and stuff them into their cheek pouches. Then they return to their underground homes and store their food in little pits in their burrows. These mammals have brownish gray grizzled fur on their backs, orange stripes down their sides, and white spiny hairs on their rumps. Their ears are big and their hind feet are long and skinny. In spring they have one litter of two to five youngsters.

FOREFOOT: SMALL BROAD PRINT; FOUR TOES

Be an ANIMAL ACE!

CALIFORNIA POCKET MICE are well adapted to their dry homes. They don't have to drink water at all—their bodies produce an internal liquid called "metabolic water."

HIND FOOT:
SMALLER CLAW MARKS;
FIVE TOES

FOREFOOT:
SHARP CLAW MARKS;
FIVE TOES

10s spotters

Plains Pocket Gopher

Geomys bursarius LENGTH 7–14 in (17.8–35.5 cm) • RANGE Central U.S. from North Dakota to Texas • HABITAT Grasslands, roadsides, fields • FOOD Roots, bulbs, green plants • ACTIVE 🅱 🅛

A Plains Pocket Gopher's "pockets" are on its cheeks. This burrowing rodent uses its front paws to shove roots and bulbs into furry pouches on the sides of its face. When these pouches are full and bulging, the gopher squeezes the food out again with its paws. Plains Pocket Gophers are built for underground life. Their brownish fur ranges from dark to pale, depending on the color of the soil around them. Their front legs are strong, with big claws for digging. They have tiny eyes and ears, but their front teeth are large and sharp. Plains Pocket Gophers spend most of their time alone and below ground, living in long burrows topped by big mounds. They have one litter each year of one to seven young.

→ **LOOK FOR THIS** *Thwip!* That plant just disappeared into the ground! That's a sign that a **POCKET GOPHER** is feeding just below. These rodents grab plants by the roots and pull them down into their burrows to eat.

HIND FOOT:
LONG WIDE PRINT;
ONE SHORT AND FOUR LONG TOES

Woodland Jumping Mouse

Napaeozapus insignis LENGTH 8–10 in (20.3–25.5 cm) • RANGE Great Lakes, northeastern U.S. to the Appalachians, Canada • HABITAT Cool, damp woods • FOOD Seeds, fungi, berries, insects • ACTIVE 🅝 🅛

10s spotters

FOREFOOT:
SMALL PRINT;
FOUR WIDE CLAW MARKS

Using their long hind feet and widespread toes, these little rodents can jump as high as 12 feet (3.5 m). Their long tails trail behind them, tipped with white. They are colorful creatures with brown backs, orange sides, and white bellies. Living in shady woods, they dig burrows and snack on seeds and underground fungi. From fall through spring they hibernate, living off the fat they built up in warm months. In summer they have one litter of two to seven young.

Meadow Jumping Mouse

Zapus hudsonius LENGTH 7.5–10 in (19–25.5 cm) • RANGE
Central and eastern U.S., Canada • HABITAT Fields, marshes,
woods • FOOD Seeds, fungi, berries, insects • ACTIVE 🌙 🌗

Surprise a Meadow Jumping
Mouse and it may leap away in a
zigzag path, jumping two or
three feet (0.6–0.9 m) at a time.
Like their cousins the Woodland
Jumping Mice, these rodents
have long hind legs and big feet
that help them spring into the air.
They have brown backs, yellow sides,
and pale bellies. Their skinny tails can be
up to six inches (15 cm) long. In warm weather,
Meadow Jumping Mice scout about in the grass for seeds
and berries. In winter, they curl up in a warm nest to
hibernate. Females give birth to one or two litters of
three to seven young each summer.

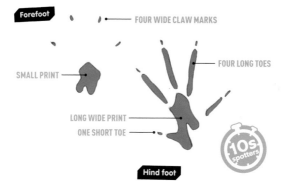

Forefoot

FOUR WIDE CLAW MARKS

FOUR LONG TOES

SMALL PRINT

LONG WIDE PRINT

ONE SHORT TOE

10s. spotters

Hind foot

EXPERT'S CIRCLE

DON'T BE FOOLED Although they both have superlong tails and hind feet, **Meadow Jumping Mice** don't have a white-tipped tail and orange-shaded coat like **Woodland Jumping Mice** (opposite). Look for a dark band down the meadow mouse's back.

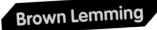

Brown Lemming

Lemmus trimucronatus LENGTH 5–7 in (12.7–17.8 cm)
• RANGE Alaska, Canada • HABITAT Wet tundra, high meadows
• FOOD Grasses, moss • ACTIVE ⏺ ⓛ

These stout little mammals are natives of the Alaska tundra, where no trees grow and where the soil goes from wet on top to frozen underground. They are stocky rodents with reddish brown fur on top and paler fur on their bellies. Their ears are tiny and their tails are stubby. They are active day and night searching for grass and moss to eat, resting every few hours in grassy nests. These lemmings are famous for their rapidly rising and falling numbers. The females can give birth by the time they are two weeks old. In one year, they can have dozens of youngsters, so over a few years lemming populations grow so fast that the animals run out of food. Then, their numbers drop quickly as they die off and the cycle starts all over again.

Be an ANIMAL ACE!

Some stories say that migrating lemmings will jump off cliffs. This doesn't happen. However, lemmings in Europe sometimes travel in big groups that run right into the sea.

Forefoot

FOUR LONG TOES

FIVE TOES

Hind foot

SMALL PRINT

NARROW PRINT

Rock Vole

Microtus chrotorrhinus LENGTH 6–7 in (15–17.8 cm) · RANGE **Northeastern U.S., Appalachians, Canada** · HABITAT **Moist, rocky hills and woods** · FOOD **Berries, green plants, fungi, insects** · ACTIVE 🅑 🅛

The Rock Vole is also known as the Yellow-nosed Vole. Both names suit it well. It lives among the rocks on damp hillsides in the Northeast. It also has a yellowish orange nose. Rock Voles are small, sleek rodents with yellowish brown fur on their backs and gray fur on their bellies. They are shy creatures. Though they are out and around day and night, collecting berries and grass to eat, you won't see them easily. They live part of the time in tunnels and also build grassy nests. Females have two to three litters a year of two to five babies apiece.

FOREFOOT: SMALL PRINT; FOUR LONG, WIDESPREAD TOES

HIND FOOT: SMALL PRINT; FIVE LONG, WIDESPREAD TOES

EXPERT'S CIRCLE

DON'T BE FOOLED On first glance, **voles** and **mice** (pages 45–47) look alike. However, voles have bigger heads and smaller eyes and ears than mice. Their legs and tails are typically short. Voles won't live in houses. They like the outdoors, where they make paths of flattened grass to their nests or tunnels.

HIND FOOT: SMALL PRINT; FIVE LONG, WIDESPREAD TOES

Prairie Vole

Microtus ochrogaster LENGTH 5–7 in (12.7–17.8 cm) · RANGE **Central U.S., Canada** · HABITAT **Prairies, grasslands, farms** · FOOD **Grass, green plants, insects** · ACTIVE 🅑 🅛

In the prairies of the central United States, the Prairie Vole lives in a grassy paradise. Scampering back and forth through the fields, it collects green plants to build into a nest, and also to eat. Prairie Voles have grizzled brown or gray fur with paler sides and bellies. Their eyes are small and tails are short. Scientists like to study Prairie Voles because they are monogamous—females and males mate for life, which is unusual in the animal world. The males help bring up the young, and there are a lot of them! These voles have several litters throughout the year, each one with three or four babies.

FOREFOOT: SMALL PRINT; FOUR LONG, WIDESPREAD TOES

Meadow Vole

Microtus pennsylvanicus LENGTH 6–8 in (15–20.3 cm) ▪ RANGE
Northeastern and north-central U.S., Canada ▪ HABITAT Meadows, grassy
fields, yards ▪ FOOD Grass, green plants, roots ▪ ACTIVE ☀ 🌙

Meadow Voles, widespread across
the northern United States, are a
favorite food for many animal predators. Foxes, hawks, owls, house cats,
snakes, Coyotes, and more snatch them
out of their grassy homes. To survive as
a species, these voles have many young.
In one year, a Meadow Vole can have up to
13 litters of 1 to 11 youngsters. Meadow Voles
have thick brown fur on their backs and pale
gray fur on their bellies. Their ears are small,
but their tails are longer than those of most
voles. They live in burrows and in grassy nests
on the ground.

→ **LOOK FOR THIS** Live in the
northern United States and not sure
if you have voles in your yard? Wait
until the snow first melts in the
spring. Look for paths in the brown
grass, marked by grassy domes.
These are the **MEADOW VOLES'**
wintertime roads and homes, which
they build between the snow and
the ground.

Forefoot

FOUR LONG,
WIDESPREAD TOES

SMALL PRINT

10s
spotters

Hind foot

FIVE LONG, WIDESPREAD TOES

SMALL PRINT

Woodland Vole

Microtus pinetorum LENGTH 4–6 in (10.2–15 cm) • RANGE
Central and eastern U.S. • HABITAT Woods with thick ground
cover • FOOD Roots, green plants, seeds • ACTIVE ⬤ ⬤

Scraping with its front feet and
teeth, and kicking out the dirt
with its hind feet, the Woodland
Vole digs shallow tunnels to
live in. Busy day and night, it collects roots and grasses to eat.
Sometimes Woodland Voles gnaw on
potato plants or apple trees, earning
the nicknames "potato mouse" or "apple
mouse." They are sleek little rodents with soft
reddish brown fur above and pale fur below. Their tails are
short and their eyes and ears are small. In all but the coldest
months, they give birth to one to four litters of one to six
young each. They often live in colonies, with several families
packing into the burrows. There they raise their youngsters
in grass-lined underground nests.

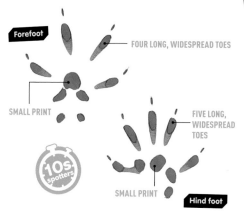

Forefoot

FOUR LONG, WIDESPREAD TOES

SMALL PRINT

FIVE LONG,
WIDESPREAD
TOES

10s
spotters

SMALL PRINT

Hind foot

EXPERT'S CIRCLE

DON'T BE FOOLED

Burrowing little **voles** can look
a lot like burrowing little **moles**
(pages 74–75). Sometimes moles
even use the same tunnels as
voles. So what's the difference?
Moles belong to a different order
of mammals. They typically have
longer, more naked noses than
voles. Moles have huge front feet,
the better to dig with. Voles are
good diggers, but their front feet
are small.

Southern Red-backed Vole

Myodes gapperi LENGTH 5–6 in (12.7–15 cm) ◦ RANGE Northern U.S. into the Rockies and Appalachians, Canada ◦ HABITAT Forests, meadows, swamps ◦ FOOD Seeds, nuts, berries, fungi ◦ ACTIVE Ⓝ Ⓛ

10s spotters

The Southern Red-backed Vole is actually a northern animal, living near the Canadian border and into western and eastern mountains.

It has this name because it lives farther south than the Northern Red-backed Vole, an Arctic animal. Southern Red-backed Voles usually do have red backs, with a broad red-brown stripe running from head to rump, though some are grayish. Their undersides are pale and their tails are short and skinny. These forest animals travel along runways and burrows built by other rodents and build round nests from grass and leaves. They raise their families in these nests, giving birth to two or three litters a year of four to five young.

FOREFOOT:
SMALL PRINT;
FOUR LONG,
WIDESPREAD TOES

Round-tailed Muskrat

FOREFOOT:
SHORT PRINT;
FOUR TOES WITH
CLAW MARKS

Neofiber alleni LENGTH 11–15 in (28–38 cm) ◦ RANGE Florida and southern Georgia ◦ HABITAT Marshes ◦ FOOD Water plants, including grasses ◦ ACTIVE Ⓝ Ⓛ

Like its bigger cousin the Common Muskrat, the Round-tailed Muskrat is basically a vole that lives in the water. Larger than regular voles, Round-tailed Muskrats have shiny brown fur with pale undersides and long, rounded, almost hairless tails. Their eyes and ears are small. These rodents are found only in warm shallow marshes in Florida and southern Georgia. There, they build round homes out of grass, with underwater entrances. These clever builders also make thick platforms from grass, rising out of the water, on which they perch to eat. Though they are mostly nighttime animals, you may see them swimming about in the day or twilight as well. They give birth to four or five litters of one to four young throughout the year.

10s spotters

HIND FOOT:
LONG PRINT;
FIVE TOES WITH
CLAW MARKS

Common Muskrat

Ondatra zibethicus **LENGTH 16–24 in (40.5–61 cm)**
RANGE Canada, U.S. except for Florida and desert
Southwest ○ **HABITAT Marshes, ponds, lakes, rivers** ○ **FOOD**
Water plants, crayfish, fish, frogs, clams ○ **ACTIVE** 🌙 🌓

The Common Muskrat is truly a creature of the water. It can swim forward and backward and stay underwater for 15 minutes at a time. Its hind feet are partly webbed and its hairless tail is flat from side to side, which helps it swim and steer. The Common Muskrat has dense, shiny fur—dark brown above and pale below—and small eyes and ears. These large rodents can be found in fresh waters across most of the United States. Typically, you see them at night or at dusk, darting through the water to find cattails, rushes, or crayfish to eat. Muskrats build their own big houses and feeding platforms from cattails and grasses. Inside, they give birth to as many as five litters of four to eight young each year.

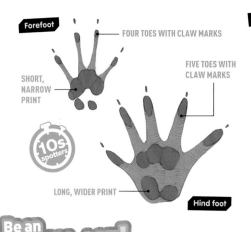

Forefoot
FOUR TOES WITH CLAW MARKS
SHORT, NARROW PRINT
FIVE TOES WITH CLAW MARKS
LONG, WIDER PRINT
Hind foot

10S spotters

EXPERT'S CIRCLE

DON'T BE FOOLED

People sometimes mistake **Common Muskrats** for American Beavers. Both are furry rodents that swim through ponds and build houses for their families. However, Common Muskrats are only about half the size of **American Beavers** (page 41). Muskrat tails are narrower and more of their bodies appear above water as they swim. Muskrat houses are smaller than beaver lodges, too, and are made from grasses and rushes, not branches.

Be an ANIMAL ACE!

Muskrat fur is shiny and warm, so muskrats are often trapped and killed for their fur. Royal Canadian Mounted Police, called Mounties, have muskrat-fur winter hats.

**HIND FOOT:
SMALL PRINT;
FIVE LONG, WIDESPREAD TOES**

Western Heather Vole

Phenacomys intermedius LENGTH 5–6 in (12.7–15 cm) ◦ RANGE Canada, Northern California, and Rockies into New Mexico ◦ HABITAT High forests and meadows, shrublands, rocky areas ◦ FOOD Bark, berries, seeds, leaves, lichens ◦ ACTIVE 🌙 🌘

**10s.
spotters**

These shy little rodents live high in the western mountains, coming out at dusk. They have grizzled brown-gray fur, white feet, short tails, and long whiskers. In the summer, they nest underground, stashing their food of bark and berries by the entrance to their tunnels. In winter, they make paths through the grass under the snow and snuggle in grassy nests. Western Heather Voles aren't sociable animals. Males drive away other males during mating season, and females fight other females for nesting territory. They have up to three litters each summer of two to nine young.

**FOREFOOT:
SMALL PRINT;
FOUR LONG, WIDESPREAD TOES**

....

Southern Bog Lemming

Synaptomys cooperi LENGTH 5–6 in (12.7–15 cm) ◦ RANGE Central and eastern U.S., Canada ◦ HABITAT Grassy meadows, forests, bogs ◦ FOOD Grasses, clover, berries, fungi ◦ ACTIVE 🌙 🌘

**HIND FOOT: LONGER PRINT;
FIVE TOES WITH CLAW PRINTS**

**10s.
spotters**

These little rodents are widespread across the eastern and central United States, but you will rarely see one. They are uncommon in many parts of their range and come out mostly at dusk and dawn. Though they're called bog lemmings—a bog is a wet spongy area—they live mostly in meadows. Southern Bog

**FOREFOOT: SMALL PRINT;
FOUR TOES WITH
CLAW PRINTS**

→ LOOK FOR THIS It may be hard to spot a **SOUTHERN BOG LEMMING,** but it's easier to spot its colorful scat—in other words, its poop. Look for piles of bright green pellets in the grass.

Lemmings have grizzled brownish fur, short stubby tails, and large heads with small eyes and ears. They make paths through the grass and shallow burrows underground, which include nesting areas lined with soft grass. Females have several litters a year of one to eight young.

Eastern Woodrat

Neotoma floridana LENGTH 12–17 in (30.5–43 cm)
• RANGE Eastern and south-central U.S. • HABITAT Rocky
areas, hedges, woods • FOOD Green plants, seeds, fruit, nuts,
fungi • ACTIVE 🌙 🌗

Eastern Woodrats are enthusiastic builders, making sturdy houses out of piled-up sticks. In the North, you can find these homes in caves or under rocks, and in the South in hedges or trees. Sometimes the woodrats even build homes inside cars or cabins, tearing up furniture and making a mess. When one woodrat moves out of a nest, another one will often move in, adding more sticks until the house can be three feet (0.9 m) high. Eastern Woodrats are medium-size rodents, gray or brown on top, with white feet and bellies and large eyes and ears. They live by themselves or with their young, which are born in litters of one to six young, two or three times a year.

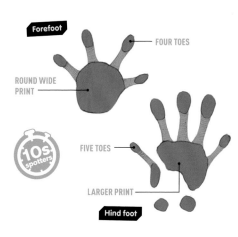

Forefoot

FOUR TOES

ROUND WIDE PRINT

10s spotters

FIVE TOES

LARGER PRINT

Hind foot

NAME GAME

Maybe you've heard some people called "pack rats" because they collect things they don't need. Woodrats are the real thing. When these pack rats, as they're often known, collect food to bring back to their houses, they sometimes collect other items as well. They particularly like shiny things, such as spoons, car parts, or jewelry. Another nickname, "trade rat," refers to their habit of dropping one item to pick up another, as if the animal is trading the first one for the second one.

HIND FOOT:
LARGER PRINT;
FIVE TOES

10s
spotters

FOREFOOT:
ROUND, WIDE PRINT;
FOUR TOES

Bushy-tailed Woodrat

Neotoma cinerea LENGTH 11–19 in (28–48.5 cm) • RANGE Canada, western U.S., California to Nebraska and New Mexico • HABITAT Rocky areas, caves, cliffs • FOOD Green plants, seeds, fruit, nuts, fungi • ACTIVE N L

Bushy-tailed Woodrats have long, flat, bushy tails like squirrels. Living in cold areas, these large rodents have thick fur, brownish to gray-ish on top and pale below. Their ears are big, thin, and shell-like. Like their cousins the Eastern Woodrats, they are "pack rats." They store shiny bits like plants and pieces of foil in their dens built from sticks in caves and rock piles. They pile the trea-sures into a heap called a midden, then pee on it. Minerals in their pee dry out and the midden gets hard. Bushy-tailed Woodrats breed once or twice a year, having two to six young each time.

Be an ANIMAL ACE!

Woodrats have lived in North America—and collected stuff—for tens of thousands of years. Plants and bones found in ancient, hardened middens give scientists valuable clues to life in prehistoric times.

HIND FOOT:
LONG PRINT;
FIVE TOES WITH CLAWS

10s
spotters

FOREFOOT:
SMALL PRINT;
FOUR TOES
WITH CLAWS

Golden Mouse

Ochrotomys nuttalli LENGTH 5–7.5 in (12.7–19 cm) • RANGE Southeastern U.S., except extreme southern Louisiana and southern Florida • HABITAT Brushy woods, vines, swamps • FOOD Nuts, seeds, berries, insects • ACTIVE N L

These pretty mice live in trees, like little monkeys. Like monkeys, they can even hold onto branches with their prehensile tails. Golden Mice have soft, golden brown fur above and white fur on their bellies and feet. Using leaves and grass, they build ball-shaped nests above the ground in vines and trees. They may also build feeding platforms where they sit to eat their food. Many golden mice may share a nest, except when a female is raising young. This happens several times a year, when the female produces a litter of one to four babies.

Northern Grasshopper Mouse

Onychomys leucogaster LENGTH 5–7.5 in (12.7–19 cm) • RANGE Western U.S., Canada • HABITAT Deserts, grasslands • FOOD Insects, lizards, seeds • ACTIVE N L

Grasshopper mice are fierce! These sturdy little rodents are excellent hunters. As their name suggests, they often catch and eat grasshoppers. They also feed on beetles, caterpillars, and spiders. Northern Grasshopper Mice are gray or brown on top and white on their bellies and feet. Their tails are short and white tufts of fur decorate the base of their ears. They have long toes and claws, the better to hold their wriggling prey.

HIND FOOT:
WIDER PRINT;
FIVE TOES WITH
BIG CLAWS

FOREFOOT:
SMALL PRINT;
FOUR TOES WITH
BIG CLAWS

These mice live in burrows with nests at their centers. They actively defend their homes against outsiders, and they will kill other mice or even rats that intrude. Females and males tend to partner for life and raise their young, which are born in several litters of one to six babies each year.

FOREFOOT:
SMALL PRINT;
FOUR TOES WITH BIG CLAWS

Southern Grasshopper Mouse

Onychomys torridus LENGTH 5–6 in (12.7–15 cm) • RANGE Southwest • HABITAT Low deserts • FOOD Insects, mice, seeds • ACTIVE N L

Like its cousin the Northern Grasshopper Mouse, the Southern Grasshopper Mouse is a predator. These stocky desert mice are grayish or golden brown above and white on their bellies; their short tails have white tips. They are sometimes known as "scorpion mice" because they are excellent scorpion hunters, holding down the scorpions' deadly tails to protect themselves while they kill it. If they catch a stinky beetle, they jam the beetle's abdomen into the ground, keeping its smelly spray from getting on their fur, before they kill it.

HIND FOOT:
WIDER PRINT;
FIVE TOES WITH
BIG CLAWS

Like Northern Grasshopper Mice, they will also kill other mice, sneaking up on them from behind and biting them in the head. These mice live in burrows, and like their Northern cousins they mate for life, giving birth to several litters of one to five young each summer.

Brush Deermouse

FOREFOOT:
SMALL PRINT;
FOUR TOES WITH CLAWS

10s spotters

HIND FOOT:
LONGER PRINT;
FIVE TOES WITH CLAWS

Peromyscus boylii LENGTH 7–9 in (17.8–23 cm) • RANGE West, Southwest • HABITAT Dry woods, brushland, high rocky areas • FOOD Seeds, nuts, berries, insects • ACTIVE N L

Deermice don't look like deer, but they move like them. They are fine jumpers and swift runners. The Brush Deermouse, a native of the high West, is a good example. It darts up trees and dashes along cliffs, using its long, tufted tail for balance. This medium-size mouse is grayish brown on top and white on its belly. A yellow-orange patch runs along its sides. Brush Deermice live in nests of dried grass under shrubs or rocks. Several times a year, females give birth to litters of two to five young.

White-footed Deermouse

HIND FOOT:
LONGER PRINT;
FIVE TOES WITH CLAWS

10s spotters

FOREFOOT:
SMALL PRINT;
FOUR TOES
WITH CLAWS

Peromyscus leucopus LENGTH 5–8 in (12.7–20.3 cm) • RANGE Central and eastern U.S., except extreme Southeast • HABITAT Woods, brushy areas, fields • FOOD Nuts, seeds, insects, fruit • ACTIVE N L

The White-footed Deermouse is common in the East. Even so, most people may never have seen one because these mice are active at night and like to hide under brush and logs. As their name suggests, they have white feet, as well as white bellies. On top, they are brown or orangey brown. Their tails have thin hairs, and their ears are big. White-footed Deermice are good climbers. They often build their nests in trees, taking over abandoned birds' nests. They also make homes inside logs or even buildings. Good swimmers, they have been found on many islands. From spring through fall, they have several litters of three to five youngsters.

DANGER!

White-footed Deermice carry deer ticks, which can give you Lyme disease. White-footed Deermice live under shrubs and in tall grasses, often near oak trees with acorns. Wear long pants and socks when you go into fields and woods, and spray your shoes and ankles with insect repellent.

North American Deermouse

Peromyscus maniculatus LENGTH 5–9 in (12.7–23 cm) · RANGE **Canada, most of the U.S. except extreme Southeast** · HABITAT **Depends on location: Woods, prairies, swamps** · FOOD **Nuts, seeds, berries, insects** · ACTIVE N L

North American Deermice are among the most common and widespread mammals in the United States. They can live almost anywhere: in woods, cliffs, swamps, or deserts. Across the country, these mice come in different colors and sizes, depending upon their habitat. Usually, they have grayish to reddish brown fur on their backs and white bellies. Their tails have short hairs with a tuft on the end. Those living in woodlands tend to have longer tails and bigger ears than those living in grasslands. They build nests in logs, abandoned burrows, or sheds, and raise several litters a year of three to five young.

HIND FOOT: LONGER PRINT; FIVE TOES WITH CLAWS

FOREFOOT: SMALL PRINT; FOUR TOES WITH CLAWS

TRY THIS!

Even experts have trouble telling one species of deermouse from another. Can you do it? Name these four deermice, based on these characteristics:

A. Tail with thin hairs, white feet

B. Huge ears

C. Long tail, orangish sides

D. Tail with a tuft at the tip

A: White-footed Deermouse (page 58)
B: Piñon Deermouse (page 59)
C: Brush Deermouse (page 58)
D: North American Deermouse (page 59)

Piñon Deermouse

FOREFOOT: SMALL PRINT; FOUR TOES WITH CLAWS

Peromyscus truei LENGTH 7–9 in (17.8–23 cm) · RANGE **Western and southwestern U.S.** · HABITAT **Dry, rocky areas with piñon pines or juniper trees** · FOOD **Piñon nuts, juniper seeds, leaves, insects** · ACTIVE N L

If you're out walking in dry western lands and you spot a pile of piñon nuts or juniper seeds, a Piñon Deermouse may be nearby. This deermouse loves these foods, and it's good at climbing trees to get at them. The Piñon Deermouse has a gray or brown back and a white belly. Its ears are huge—about as long as its hind feet. It scouts for food at night and nests inside hollow trees or under rocks in the day. From spring through fall, it has several litters of three to six young.

HIND FOOT: LONGER PRINT; FIVE TOES WITH CLAWS

Marsh Rice Rat

Oryzomys palustris LENGTH 7.5–12 in (19–30.5 cm) • RANGE Southeastern U.S., Atlantic coast up to New Jersey • HABITAT Marshes, riverbanks • FOOD Insects, fish, other small animals, plants • ACTIVE N L

Floods? Rivers? No problem! The Marsh Rice Rat is a fine swimmer. These mammals spend much of their time in the water, looking for food and escaping land-bound enemies. Their fur, grayish brown on top and pale below, keeps out the water. Their tails are long and mostly hairless, and their eyes and ears are medium-size. They are eager meat-eaters, snacking on crabs, snails, fish, and other small animals, but they will also eat rice or plants. Marsh Rice Rats build their grassy nests above the water and sometimes take over bird nests or muskrat lodges. They have several litters of four to six young each year.

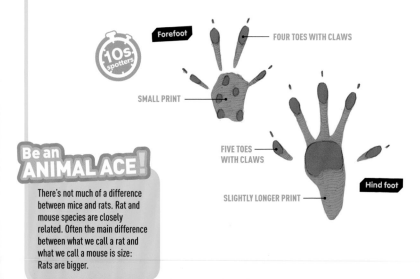

10s spotters

Forefoot FOUR TOES WITH CLAWS

SMALL PRINT

FIVE TOES WITH CLAWS

SLIGHTLY LONGER PRINT

Hind foot

Be an ANIMAL ACE!

There's not much of a difference between mice and rats. Rat and mouse species are closely related. Often the main difference between what we call a rat and what we call a mouse is size: Rats are bigger.

Eastern Harvest Mouse

Reithrodontomys humulis LENGTH 4–6 in (10.2–15 cm)
• RANGE Southeastern U.S. north to Ohio and west to Texas
• HABITAT Meadows, brushy areas, marshes • FOOD Seeds, green plants, insects • ACTIVE 🌙 🌗

Even by mouse standards, these mice are small. Eastern Harvest Mice are tiny rodents, with reddish brown upper fur and pale sides. Their bellies are gray and their tails are almost hairless. They are well named because they do "harvest" seeds from crops and grasses, storing them in their small, round nests. They give birth to several litters of three to five young from spring to fall. Like other mice, they are a main source of food for many predators, including owls, foxes, and Coyotes.

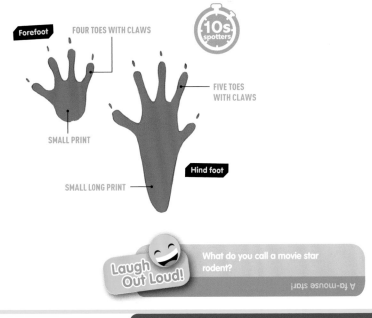

Forefoot
FOUR TOES WITH CLAWS
FIVE TOES WITH CLAWS
SMALL PRINT
Hind foot
SMALL LONG PRINT

10s spotters

Laugh Out Loud!
What do you call a movie star rodent?

A fa-mouse star!

Hispid Cotton Rat

Sigmodon hispidus LENGTH 8–15 in (20.3–38 cm) · RANGE Southeastern and south-central U.S. · HABITAT Grasslands, fields · FOOD Grasses, green plants, insects, eggs · ACTIVE 🅑 🅛

Hispid Cotton Rats like warm places. As many as 30 per acre (70 per hectare) will live in southern fields in late summer, when the pickings are good. Farmers don't want them around because they eat crops, including sugarcane and sweet potatoes. These medium-size rats have grizzled tan or gray fur on their backs and creamy fur on their bellies. Their short tails are mostly hairless. They make long paths through the grass and build woven nests, where they give birth year-round. Females can have up to 15 young in each litter.

HIND FOOT:
SMALL WIDE PRINT;
FIVE TOES WITH
CLAWS

Black Rat

FOREFOOT:
SMALL WIDE PRINT;
FOUR TOES WITH CLAWS

Rattus rattus LENGTH 13–18 in (33–46 cm) · RANGE East and West Coasts, southern U.S., Canada · HABITAT Buildings, ships, coastal woods and fields · FOOD Grains, seeds, fruit, garbage · ACTIVE 🅝 🅛

The Black Rat is also known as the Ship Rat or Roof Rat, and those names may suit it better. It is not native to North America: The first Black Rats arrived on sailing ships with the first colonists. They still like to live on ships and in shipyards and are good at climbing into the roof rafters of coastal buildings. Black Rats may be black or brown or gray, with gray underparts. Their tails are long and mostly hairless. They eat almost anything but prefer grain, and they can do great damage to crops and grain storehouses. They breed year-round, with litters of two to eight young.

HIND FOOT:
LONG FLAT PRINT;
FIVE TOES WITH CLAWS

Be an ANIMAL ACE!

Black Rats, Norway Rats, and House Mice are all Old World rodents: They came to North America aboard ships from Europe. They are very adaptable and successful animals. However, they are not popular with humans because they get into our buildings and into our food, and they spread disease.

Norway Rat

Rattus norvegicus LENGTH 12–18 in (30.5–46 cm)
• RANGE Southern Canada, entire U.S. • HABITAT Cities, suburbs, fields, marshes • FOOD Grains, seeds, fruit, meat, garbage • ACTIVE **N** **L**

The Norway Rat is one of the most successful mammals on the planet. It lives not only everywhere in North America but also everywhere around the world except for the high Arctic and Antarctica. Brought to the United States aboard ships during the American Revolution, this rodent has easily adapted to living in cities and suburbs. It is not a popular animal! Norway Rats chew up buildings, get into kitchens, and can carry diseases. These rats are brown on top and grayish below. Their tails are fairly short and hairless and their eyes are small. Excellent diggers and swimmers, they make their way through sewers and will carve out tunnels in which to live and breed. They are sociable animals and can live in large groups, with one male taking charge. Female Norway Rats give birth to many litters of 7 to 11 young apiece throughout the year.

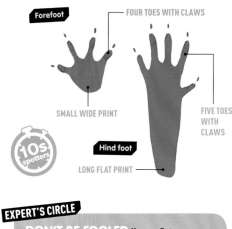

Forefoot — FOUR TOES WITH CLAWS

SMALL WIDE PRINT

FIVE TOES WITH CLAWS

Hind foot

LONG FLAT PRINT

10s spotters

NAME GAME

The Norway Rat does not come from Norway—but the first biologist to give it its scientific name thought it did. Norway Rats probably started out in China before they began to hitch rides aboard ships and caravans around the world. They are also known as Brown Rats, Common Rats, Water Rats, and Sewer Rats.

EXPERT'S CIRCLE

DON'T BE FOOLED **Norway Rats** are browner, with bigger bodies and shorter tails than **Black Rats** (opposite). Native woodrats have white bellies.

MAMMAL MANIA:
CITY CRITTERS

A RACCOON RAIDS A GARBAGE CAN ON A SUMMER NIGHT.

Crammed with buildings and busy with traffic and crowds, cities don't seem like they would be home to wild animals, but that's not the case. Many animals, including mammals, live and breed under city streets, in sewers, and in parks and buildings. Some, such as squirrels, are familiar daytime creatures. Others rule the night: raccoons, deer, bats, foxes, and more. The truth is that people in cities are outnumbered by other mammals, big and small.

Oh, Rats!

Some mammals don't just live in cities: They truly thrive there. The best and most unpopular examples are Norway Rats (page 63). These rodents eat what people eat—especially food high in fat and protein, like pizza. They can climb walls, fit through holes the size of a quarter, and swim through sewers. They can even swim up through toilets. New York City alone has two million rats!

Wily Coyotes

Other mammals have adapted well to cities but are still a bit shy and wild. For example, in recent years many city dwellers have been surprised to see Coyotes (page 106) in their parks, cemeteries, and even on rooftops. Trotting about by day and night, Coyotes mostly eat smaller animals, but also human food. They've learned to drink from swimming pools and look for traffic before crossing streets. Sometimes city people hear them howling at night.

Mountain Lion in Wait

As cities grow into the country around them, they invade the natural range of some wild mammals. Big predators, such as Mountain Lions (page 103), need a lot of room in which to hunt and raise families. In recent years, Mountain Lions have been seen around the edges of some big cities. Sometimes they are following their prey, such as deer, into crowded areas. One Mountain Lion was even spotted in front of the Hollywood sign in Los Angeles.

House Mouse

Mus musculus LENGTH **5–8 in (12.7–20.3 cm)** ▪ RANGE
Canada, entire U.S. ▪ HABITAT **Fields, buildings** ▪ FOOD **Seeds,
grain, insects, human food** ▪ ACTIVE **N L**

Like the Norway Rat, the House
Mouse came to North America
aboard settlers' ships from
Europe. Now this very successful
little rodent has spread throughout the country. It likes farm fields,
where thousands can live and feed
during harvest time. True to their names,
House Mice also do well in buildings. They can
squeeze through tiny openings and live in walls, furniture, or in
burrows under floors. House Mice are small, with short brownish
gray fur and hairless ears and tails. They live in colonies, where
they share eating spaces with other House Mice. Females spend
most of their short lives raising babies. They have up to 14 litters
a year, with 3 to 12 youngsters in each.

Be an ANIMAL ACE!

The House Mouse is one of the
most studied animals on Earth.
In laboratory work, the white
mice are House Mice and the
white rats are Norway Rats.

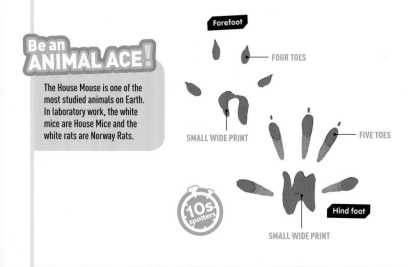

Forefoot

FOUR TOES

SMALL WIDE PRINT

FIVE TOES

Hind foot

SMALL WIDE PRINT

10S spotters

Nutria

Myocastor coypus LENGTH 2–4.6 ft (0.6–1.4 m) • RANGE Gulf Coast, scattered in southeastern and western U.S. • HABITAT Streams, rivers, marshes • FOOD Water plants, grains • ACTIVE ◑ ◐

Nutrias, also called Coypus, are native to South America and the Caribbean. Fur farmers brought them to the United States in the 1930s, but the animals soon escaped and spread through the Southeast and elsewhere. They are not welcome in most places because they eat through wetlands and farmers' crops. Large, beaverlike rodents, Nutrias have yellowish brown fur, long, rounded tails, and huge orange front teeth. They are good swimmers and can stay underwater for several minutes. Nutrias don't build lodges, like beavers, but they will live in an empty beaver lodge, or else build a nest in which to raise their young. Baby nutrias are born in litters of four to six, two or three times a year.

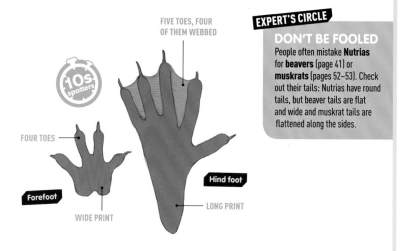

FIVE TOES, FOUR OF THEM WEBBED

FOUR TOES

10s spotters

Forefoot

WIDE PRINT

Hind foot

LONG PRINT

EXPERT'S CIRCLE

DON'T BE FOOLED

People often mistake **Nutrias** for **beavers** (page 41) or **muskrats** (pages 52–53). Check out their tails: Nutrias have round tails, but beaver tails are flat and wide and muskrat tails are flattened along the sides.

INSECTIVORES

Northern Short-tailed Shrew

Blarina brevicauda LENGTH 4–5 in (10.2–12.7 cm) • RANGE North-central and northeastern U.S., Canada • HABITAT Woods, grassy areas, marshes • FOOD Insects, worms, snails, small mammals, fungi • ACTIVE Ⓑ Ⓛ

Watch out—the Northern Short-tailed Shrew packs a mean bite! This tiny creature is one of the few venomous mammals in the world. Glands in its jaw make a poison that enters its saliva. When the shrew chomps down on a snail, insect, or mouse, the poison either paralyzes the prey or kills it. The shrew may then store its prey in its tunnels to be eaten later. Northern Short-tailed Shrews are small, with silvery gray fur above and below. Their eyes are small, their tails are short, and their ears are hidden in their fur. Like all shrews, they are fast-moving, nervous, and always hungry. Northern Short-taileds can eat more than their body weight in food every day. They live under cover in grass and leafy woods, building narrow little tunnels with soft nesting areas. Females have several litters of three to seven young each year.

→ **LOOK FOR THIS SHREWS** are small and hard to spot in the wild. Look for the small openings to their burrows, no more than one inch (2.5 cm) wide, in stream banks, under a log, or in moss.

Forefoot

FIVE TOES WITH CLAWS

FIVE TOES WITH CLAWS

TINY PRINT

Hind foot

TINY NARROW PRINT

10s spotters

DANGER! ☠

The bite of the Northern Short-tailed Shrew is poison-packed.

Least Shrew

Cryptotis parva LENGTH 3–4 in (7.5–10.2 cm) · RANGE Central and eastern U.S.
· HABITAT Fields, woods, marshes · FOOD Insects, worms, spiders · ACTIVE 🅑 🅛

Weighing less than a nickel, the tiny Least
Shrew could hide inside a teacup. What it lacks
in size, it makes up for in energy and sociabil-
ity. Active day and night finding insects to eat,
it also digs tunnels where it may live with dozens of other Least Shrews. Least Shrews have

FOREFOOT:
TINY PRINT;
FIVE TOES
WITH CLAWS

HIND FOOT:
TINY NARROW PRINT;
FIVE TOES WITH CLAWS

brownish gray fur on their backs, gray fur on their undersides, pointy
noses, and short ears and tails. They have bad eyesight, but good senses
of smell and hearing. Like other shrews,
they make quiet, high-pitched clicks that
bounce off objects and return to the
shrews' ears, helping them navigate.
They have litters of two to seven
young year-round.

The heart of an excited shrew will beat
1,200 times a minute (an adult human
heart beats 60 to 80 times a minute).

HIND FOOT:
TINY NARROW PRINT;
FIVE TOES WITH CLAWS

Arctic Shrew

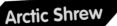

Sorex arcticus LENGTH 4–5 in (10.2–12.7 cm) · RANGE Northern plains, Canada
· HABITAT Marshes, swamps, forest clearings · FOOD Insects, insect larvae · ACTIVE 🅑 🅛

The Arctic Shrew is also known as the Saddle-
backed Shrew because of the dark brown
saddle-shaped patch that runs along its back.
Its fur actually has three colors: dark brown
on its back, light brown on its sides, and pale
gray on its belly. It has small eyes and ears
and a pointy nose. The Arctic Shrew is a creature of cold climates, and like all shrews it is
on the move day and night to eat and keep up its
energy. Females have several litters of four to eight
youngsters throughout the summer. It's a tough
life for the little animals: Eight out of every ten
will die before they are grown.

FOREFOOT:
TINY PRINT;
FIVE TOES WITH CLAWS

Pacific Water Shrew

FOREFOOT:
TINY PRINT;
FIVE TOES WITH CLAWS

Sorex bendirii **LENGTH 6–7 in (15–17.8 cm)** ▪ **RANGE Washington State to Northern California, Canada** ▪ **HABITAT Streams, marshes** ▪ **FOOD Insect larvae, insects, worms** ▪ **ACTIVE N L**

When it has to, the Pacific Water Shrew can run on top of the water, thanks to air trapped in the hairs of its feet—a natural flotation device. It's also a good diver and swims quickly searching for water insects to eat. Air bubbles in its dense fur make it look silvery underwater. Compared with other shrews, the Pacific Water Shrew is pretty big, about the size of a mouse. Dark brown all over, it has a long tail and a long, whiskered nose. Not much is known about how often it breeds. Although they are not endangered, Pacific Water Shrews are fairly rare and you'll be lucky to spot one in its marshy home.

HIND FOOT:
TINY NARROW PRINT;
FIVE TOES WITH CLAWS

Rock Shrew

HIND FOOT:
TINY NARROW PRINT;
FIVE TOES WITH CLAWS

Sorex dispar **LENGTH 4–5.5 in (10.2–14 cm)** ▪ **RANGE Eastern U.S., Maine to North Carolina** ▪ **HABITAT Rocky areas** ▪ **FOOD Insects, spiders, centipedes** ▪ **ACTIVE B L**

You'll have to be very patient to spot the Rock Shrew. True to its name, it lives under and between rocks, mostly in the Appalachian Mountains. It rarely comes out into the open. It's also known as the Long-tailed Shrew. This long tail may help it balance as it leaps among the rocks. Dark gray on top and slightly paler below, Rock Shrews have long, skinny heads that are well shaped for poking into cracks to find food. Several times a year, these shrews have litters of four to seven young, which are raised in grassy nests.

FOREFOOT:
TINY PRINT;
FIVE TOES WITH CLAWS

EXPERT'S CIRCLE

DON'T BE FOOLED Although they belong to different animal orders, **shrews** and **mice** (like the House Mouse, page 66) look somewhat alike. You can tell them apart by their head shapes: Shrews have longer, narrower snouts. Shrews also have five toes on their front feet, while mice have four.

Masked Shrew

Sorex cinereus **LENGTH 3–4 in (7.5–10.2 cm)** ▪ **RANGE Northern U.S., Canada** ▪ **HABITAT Woods, fields, marshes, swamp** ▪ **FOOD Insects, snails, spiders** ▪ **ACTIVE** 🌙 🌓

This tiny shrew lives through-out the northern United States and across Canada. Like other shrews, though, it is rarely seen. It is shy and active mainly at night. Masked Shrews are brown above and pale below, with long, black-tipped tails. Like all shrews, they have to eat almost constantly to stay alive. Even in the cold regions in which they live, they are busy all winter hunting insects, spiders, and other little creatures. Usually, they travel under leaf litter or in tunnels and build leafy nests in which to raise their young. Females raise up to three litters of 4 to 10 young in the sum-mers. The tiny babies are about the size of a grain of rice.

Forefoot

FIVE TOES WITH CLAWS

TINY PRINT

FIVE TOES WITH CLAWS

Hind foot

TINY NARROW PRINT

Be an ANIMAL ACE!

You're not likely ever to see young shrews. The teeny young ones stay hidden in their nests until they are almost grown.

10S spotters

HIND FOOT:
TINY NARROW PRINT;
FIVE TOES WITH CLAWS

Smoky Shrew

Sorex fumeus LENGTH 4–5 in (10.2–12.7 cm) ▪ RANGE **Canada, Northeastern U.S. south through the mountains of Tennessee** ▪ HABITAT **Wet woodlands** ▪ FOOD **Insects, worms, salamanders** ▪ ACTIVE Ⓝ Ⓛ

FOREFOOT: TINY PRINT;
FIVE TOES WITH CLAWS

Smoky Shrews live in damp eastern woods, dashing about in burrows under wet leaves and old logs. In summer, they have brown fur on top and paler brown fur below. In winter, their fur changes to dark gray above and silvery below. Females give birth in their second year, having two to three litters of four to seven young in the summer. Like other shrews, Smoky Shrews live fast and die young: Their natural life span is no more than 17 months.

Be an ANIMAL ACE!

Smoky Shrews, Masked Shrews, and Northern Short-tailed Shrews sometimes live in the same territories. They can do this because they don't compete for food. Each kind of shrew eats a different-size insect or worm.

HIND FOOT:
TINY NARROW PRINT;
FIVE TOES WITH CLAWS

Merriam's Shrew

Sorex merriami LENGTH 3.5–4 in (8.9–10.2 cm) ▪ RANGE **Western U.S.** ▪ HABITAT **Dry grasslands, woods, sagebrush** ▪ FOOD **Caterpillars, beetles, other insects** ▪ ACTIVE Ⓝ Ⓛ

Merriam's Shrews live across the high, dry West, but only in spots here and there. These medium-size shrews have gray fur above, paler sides, and a whitish belly. Their tails are long and dark on top, but light below. Like other male shrews, the males' glands give off a strong, musky smell—but the odor is stinkier than most. This may attract females while driving away predators, like cats. Little is known about these shy shrews. They probably give birth in the summer, with litters of five to seven young.

FOREFOOT:
TINY PRINT;
FIVE TOES
WITH CLAWS

Laugh Out Loud!

How many shrews does it take to make a stink?

A phew!

Pacific Shrew

Sorex pacificus LENGTH 5–6 in (12.7–15 cm) • RANGE Pacific coast of Oregon and Northern California • HABITAT Wet forests, stream banks • FOOD Insects, snails, amphibians • ACTIVE N L

These shrews live only in the damp woods along the northwest Pacific coast. For shrews they are fairly large, with rich red-brown or dark brown fur above, paler orange-brown fur below, and long tails. Pacific Shrews are excellent hunters. Not only do they hunt with both sight and smell, but they seem to be able to track their prey with sound, as Least Shrews and bats do. They can catch insects flying close to the ground. Extra food is stashed near their nest to be eaten later. Females bear their young in the summer, giving birth to two to seven babies in each litter.

FOREFOOT:
TINY PRINT;
FIVE TOES WITH
CLAWS

HIND FOOT:
TINY NARROW PRINT;
FIVE TOES WITH CLAWS

HIND FOOT:
TINY NARROW PRINT;
FIVE TOES WITH CLAWS

American Water Shrew

Sorex palustris LENGTH 5.5–6 in (14–15 cm) • RANGE Canada, northern U.S. into the Appalachians, Sierras, Rocky Mountains • HABITAT Stream banks, ponds, wet areas • FOOD Insects, worms, small fish • ACTIVE B L

Like the Pacific Water Shrew, the American Water Shrew can actually walk on water, thanks to its partly webbed back feet with stiff hairs. After it dives to find food, air bubbles in its fur float it back to the surface. The American Water Shrew is fairly big for a shrew and has dark brown or black fur on top, a silvery belly, and a long tail. It is active day and night, scurrying about hunting for food, resting, then hunting again. It lives in tunnels near streams and ponds, where it builds small nests in which to raise its young. Females have two to three litters each year of 2 to 10 young apiece.

FOREFOOT:
TINY PRINT;
FIVE TOES WITH CLAWS

Be an ANIMAL ACE!

American Water Shrews, like many shrews, will fight each other fiercely. The fight begins with loud squeaks as they stand up on their hind legs. If neither one backs off, they attack each other with their sharp teeth.

10s spotters

Star-nosed Mole

Condylura cristata LENGTH 6–8 in (15–20.3 cm) ◦ RANGE Canada, northeastern U.S. to Minnesota and Georgia ◦ HABITAT Wet woods, meadows, swamps ◦ FOOD Worms, water insects ◦ ACTIVE **D** **L**

No other animal on Earth looks like the Star-nosed Mole. Sticking out of this little mammal's snout are 22 fleshy, wiggling tentacles. On them, tiny sensory buds give the mole an excellent sense of touch. The Star-nosed Mole moves through tunnels that it digs easily and quickly. They may lead right into a stream where, unlike other moles, it's a good swimmer. These moles have short, dense black fur; long, hairy tails; and big front feet with long claws. Their small ears are hidden in their fur. They have one litter per year of two to seven young.

HIND FOOT:
SMALLER PRINT;
NARROW FOOT
WITH FIVE TOES

Mammals look the way they do for a reason. Invent one in a drawing and name it. Why does it have the fur, or nose, or feet that it does? Where does it live? What does it eat? Is it nocturnal?

TRY THIS!

HIND FOOT:
SMALLER PRINT;
NARROW FOOT WITH FIVE TOES

Eastern Mole

Scalopus aquaticus LENGTH 3–9 in (7.5–23 cm) ◦ RANGE Eastern U.S. ◦ HABITAT Fields, lawns, woods ◦ FOOD Worms, insects ◦ ACTIVE **D** **L**

Eastern Moles can dig, dig, dig. Many homeowners don't like to see their shallow tunnels, with low ridges, crisscrossing a lawn. But the tunnels can help the soil, loosening it up and airing it out. Deeper tunnels hold the moles' nesting rooms. Their short fur is gray in northern moles and brown in southern and western moles. Their wide forefeet turn outward, and their short tails are naked. Living mainly underground, they don't need good vision: Their eyes are always closed. Eastern Moles have one litter each spring of two to five young.

10s spotters

FOREFOOT:
LARGER PRINT;
WIDE FOOT WITH FIVE TOES

NAME GAME

The Eastern Mole's species was named *aquaticus*, because the first one to be named was found drowned in a well.

Hairy-tailed Mole

Parascalops breweri LENGTH 5.5–7 in (14–17.8 cm) • RANGE Northeastern U.S., Canada • HABITAT Woods, fields, lawns • FOOD Worms, insects • ACTIVE 🅑 🅛

Unlike most other moles, the Hairy-tailed Mole has a short, hairy tail. Its fur is dense and grayish black above and paler below. Like all moles, it has big front feet and a naked, pointy snout. It lives in woods and meadows, where it tunnels under the leafy ground. During the day, Hairy-tails stay out of sight belowground, but at night they sometimes come out to look around for worms, grubs, and insects to eat. In winter, they dig deeper, warmer tunnels to live in. Females have one litter each year of four to five babies.

FOREFOOT: LARGER PRINT WIDE FOOT WITH FIVE TOES

HIND FOOT: SMALLER PRINT; NARROW FOOT WITH FIVE TOES

Townsend's Mole

Scapanus townsendii LENGTH 8–9 in (20.3–23 cm) • RANGE Canada, northwest coast from Washington to Northern California • HABITAT Wet fields, woods, mountain meadows • FOOD Worms, insects, plants • ACTIVE 🅝 🅛

HIND FOOT: SMALLER PRINT; NARROW FOOT WITH FIVE TOES

You won't usually see the Townsend's Mole out in the daytime, but you can certainly see where it's been digging. Like all moles, the Townsend's pushes dirt to the surface as it digs its tunnels. This dirt builds up into little mounds called mole hills. The hills of a Townsend's Mole are bigger than most, at about seven inches (17.8 cm) high, and one mole can kick up hundreds of them in a few months. The Townsend's is a big mole with shiny dark brown or black fur. It has large front paws and a narrow, hairless snout. Females give birth once a year, in spring, to two to five young.

FOREFOOT: LARGER PRINT; WIDE FOOT WITH FIVE TOES

Be an ANIMAL ACE!

Moles have silky fur that lies flat when it's pressed toward the front or the back of their bodies. This makes it easy for them to scoot forward or backward in their tight tunnels.

American Pika

Ochotona princeps LENGTH 6–9 in (15–23 cm) • RANGE Western
mountain states, Canada • HABITAT Rocky areas on mountain slopes
• FOOD Grasses, other green plants • ACTIVE ⏻ ⏾

American Pikas are small but noisy.
From their rocky ledges in western
mountains, they bark and whistle
to warn of predators or to call out
to mates. These members of the
rabbit family don't look much like
rabbits. They are plump, with orangish
or brown fur, rounded ears, and small
tails. Living in dens among the rocks, they
scurry out to gather food like little farmers.
After cutting down grasses and other green plants,
they spread them out to dry before stacking them up to eat
through the winter. Females give birth to two litters of about
three babies each per year.

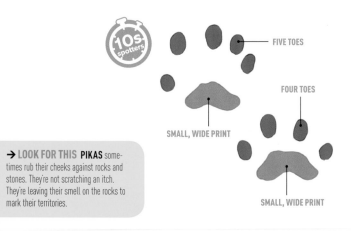

FIVE TOES

FOUR TOES

SMALL, WIDE PRINT

SMALL, WIDE PRINT

→ **LOOK FOR THIS** **PIKAS** sometimes rub their cheeks against rocks and
stones. They're not scratching an itch.
They're leaving their smell on the rocks to
mark their territories.

Pygmy Rabbit

Brachylagus idahoensis LENGTH **10–11 in (25.5–28 cm)** • RANGE
Washington, Oregon to Nevada • HABITAT **Dry, sagebrush areas** • FOOD **Sagebrush,
grasses** • ACTIVE 🌙 🌘

FOREFOOT:
SMALLER,
OVAL PRINTS
IN A LINE

HIND FOOT:
SMALL, OVAL PRINTS

This little mammal is the smallest rabbit in
North America—and the world. It lives in dry
areas of the West where sagebrush, a silvery
green shrub, grows. Pygmy Rabbits are grayish or brownish above, with pale bellies. Their
rounded ears are furry and their small tails
are gray. Unlike other rabbits, they will dig their own burrows to live in,
though they'll also take over burrows other animals have left behind.
In spring, they give birth to up to three litters of about six young
each. In Washington State, an isolated group of Pygmy Rabbits is
endangered: Fewer than 50 of these Columbia Basin Pygmy Rabbits
may still live in the wild.

HIND FOOT :
LONG, OVAL PRINTS

Black-tailed Jackrabbit

Lepus californicus LENGTH **18.5–25 in (47–63.5 cm)** • RANGE **Western and
central U.S. except northern Rockies and plains** • HABITAT **Dry prairies, meadows,
pastures** • FOOD **Grasses, shrubs, crops** • ACTIVE 🌙 🌘

FOREFOOT:
SMALLER, OVAL PRINTS
IN A LINE

Lean, speedy machines, Black-tailed
Jackrabbits are common across the dry
grasslands of the United States. They are
are also commonly known as hares. Their fur
is peppery gray or tan above and white below;
their tails have a black stripe on top, with a
white border. The black-tipped ears are up to five
inches (12.7 cm) long. Using their long, strong hind
feet, they can dash in zigzag hops at up to 35 miles
an hour (56 km/h). Every few hops will be especially
high, letting the hare see what's around it. Black-tailed Jackrabbits eat a
lot of grass, sagebrush, and even cacti. Like most hares and rabbits, they
have many babies: three or four litters a year with one to six youngsters
each. Hundreds of them can live in one square mile (2.6 sq km) of land.

MAMMAL MANIA: MAMMAL BABIES

A FAWN PAUSES IN A MEADOW IN SPRING.

Giving birth to live babies and feeding them milk is part of what makes a mammal, a mammal. Even so, mammals vary a lot in how many babies they have and how they raise them. In general, small, short-lived mammals have more babies in their litters and have litters more often. Big, longer-lived mammals tend to have fewer young, less often. Sometimes these babies are born with closed eyes and no fur. They can't survive on their own for weeks, months, or years. Others are born able to walk and find their own food almost right away.

Pups in a Pouch

Newborn Virginia Opossums (page 16), called pups, are hairless and the size of honeybees. They have strong front legs, though, which help them climb into their mother's pouch right after birth. Up to 13 at a time will ride in the pouch and drink her milk for a couple of months. After that, they may come out but will still drink the mother's milk for another month and ride on her back for up to two months more.

Rabbits, Rabbits, Rabbits

Rabbits are famous for having lots and lots of babies. One Eastern Cottontail (page 84) can give birth to 35 youngsters a year. If all the females in those litters go on to breed at the same rate, and their babies do the same, within just two years you're looking at more than a thousand rabbits. It's a tough life for the little kits, though. The reason the world is not covered with bunnies is that so many of them die young, often by becoming prey for bigger animals.

Caring for Cubs

Black Bear cubs (page 110) have a lot of growing to do. Newborns grow to 250 times their birth size by the time they are adults. If a human baby did that, it would weigh 2,000 pounds (907 kg) when it grew up! Female bears have one or two cubs at a time and take good care of them for up to two years. The mother and cubs snuggle together in their den and stay close until the youngsters can live on their own.

Water Babies

Imagine being born underwater and surrounded by danger. That's how whale babies, such as Gray Whales (page 130), come into the world. For that reason, Gray Whale calves are well developed at birth. They have good senses and are able to swim. At first, the mother may hold them on her back out of the water to breathe, but within a few days they can manage on their own. As the babies grow, the mothers feed them milk and stroke them tenderly with their flippers. Mother Grays also defend their babies fiercely against Orcas and even against boats that come too close.

Snowshoe Hare

Lepus americanus LENGTH **15–20 in (38–51 cm)** • RANGE **Canada, Alaska, northern U.S. into western mountains and Appalachians** • HABITAT **Forests, brushy areas** • FOOD **Green plants, berries, twigs, bark** • ACTIVE 🌙 🌓

As the seasons change, so does the Snowshoe Hare. In summer, its fur is brown or reddish brown. As the days grow shorter and snow starts to fall, white patches fill in until, in winter, the coat is all white. Except for its dark eyes and dark-tipped ears, the hare blends in perfectly with the snow. (In warm places, it may stay brown all year.) Snowshoe Hares are fairly small for hares. Their long hind feet have thick, stiff fur on the bottom, good for traveling on the snow. They have lots of young—up to five litters a year of one to seven babies. The numbers of Snowshoe Hares in an area go up and down in a big way, ranging from just a few in low years to thousands in high years.

Be an ANIMAL ACE!

The Canada Lynx (page 101) is one of the Snowshoe Hare's main predators. Its numbers rise and fall depending on how many hares are born the previous year. When there are lots of Snowshoe Hares one year, there are lots of well-fed Canada Lynx the next. When there are fewer Snowshoe Hares, the Canada Lynx lose their food source and their numbers drop the next year.

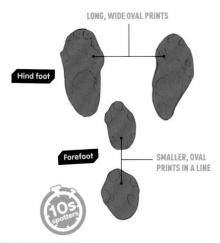

LONG, WIDE OVAL PRINTS

Hind foot

Forefoot

SMALLER, OVAL PRINTS IN A LINE

10s spotters

Antelope Jackrabbit

Lepus alleni LENGTH 22–26 in (55–66 cm) · RANGE Southern Arizona · HABITAT Dry, grassy, shrubby areas · FOOD Grasses, shrubs, cacti · ACTIVE 🌙 🌅

The Antelope Jackrabbit is one of the fastest mammals in North America. Springing forward from its long, strong hind legs, it can run as fast as 40 miles an hour (64 km/h) and jump as far as 20 feet (6 m) in a single leap. This large hare of the Southwest desert is grizzled grayish brown above and white below. Its enormous ears can be eight inches (20.3 cm) long. In summer, the hare holds them upright to release heat. In winter, it folds them down over its back to stay warm. Antelope Jackrabbits stay under cover during the hot day, coming out to eat as the sun sets. They have three or four litters of one to five young each year.

FOREFOOT: SMALLER, OVAL PRINTS

HIND FOOT: LONG OVAL PRINTS

→ LOOK FOR THIS Flash! Flash! Flash! As the **ANTELOPE JACKRABBIT** runs, it flashes a white patch of fur on its rump. This zigzag patch of white might confuse predators that are chasing it, so it can get away.

HIND FOOT: LONG OVAL PRINTS

European Hare

Lepus europaeus LENGTH 24–30 in (61–76 cm) · RANGE Great Lakes, New York, New England · HABITAT Open fields, meadows · FOOD Grasses, berries, twigs · ACTIVE 🌙 🌅

This large hare is native to Europe, but it was brought to New York in the 19th century. It has thick, curly, yellowish brown fur on top and a white belly. Its large ears have black tips. Like other hares, it is strong and quick, able to run as fast as 30 miles an hour (48 km/h). It's also a good swimmer and can easily cross a stream or small river. By day, the European Hare rests under cover. At dawn and dusk, it comes out to feed. Females have three or four litters a year, with three to five young each.

FOREFOOT: SMALLER, OVAL PRINTS

Be an ANIMAL ACE!

In the spring, male and female European Hares come out in the daytime. If the females aren't ready to mate yet, they will fight the males, with both hares standing on their hind legs and "boxing" with their front feet.

Alaska Hare

Lepus othus LENGTH **22–27 in (56–68.5 cm)** ▪ RANGE **Northern and western Alaska** ▪ HABITAT **Tundra** ▪ FOOD **Shrubs, bark, twigs, berries** ▪ ACTIVE **N** **L**

Like the Snowshoe Hare, the Alaska Hare changes color from summer to winter. In summer, this large hare has a red-brown or brown-gray coat, with a white belly. In winter, its coat becomes all white to match the snow, except for black tips on its medium-size ears. Though it lives in some of the coldest places in North America, the Alaska Hare doesn't seem to mind. It is active year-round and raises its young in open nests on the ground. Alaska Hares have just one litter per year of four to eight young.

HIND FOOT:
LONG OVAL PRINTS

FOREFOOT:
SMALLER, OVAL PRINTS

Swamp Rabbit

Sylvilagus aquaticus LENGTH **18–22 in (46–56 cm)** ▪ RANGE **South-central U.S.** ▪ HABITAT **Swamps, marshes, wet areas** ▪ FOOD **Grasses, shrubs, twigs** ▪ ACTIVE **N** **L**

This rabbit of the watery South is comfortable in wet places. It's a good swimmer and will hide in the water when in danger, with only its nose showing. Swamp Rabbits are large among rabbits, with grizzled brown fur on top and pale bellies. Their tails are short and fluffy, and they have an orange ring around each eye. Females give birth to two or three litters a year of one to six youngsters, which they raise in a shallow, fur-lined nest.

FOREFOOT:
SMALL, OVAL
PRINTS

HIND FOOT:
LONG OVAL
PRINTS

NAME GAME

People who study rabbits and hares use a special set of words to describe them. Female rabbits are does and males are bucks. Old rabbits are coneys and young ones are kits or leverets. The shallow holes they live in are called forms.

Desert Cottontail

Sylvilagus audubonii LENGTH **14–17 in (35.5–43 cm)**
· RANGE **North Dakota to Texas and west to California** · HABITAT
Deserts, grasslands · FOOD **Grasses, other green plants, twigs,
fruits** · ACTIVE ⬤ ⬤

The Desert Cottontail makes its home
among the grasses and shrubs of the
dry western states. During the day, it
rests among the plants. In the evening, it
comes out to look for the grasses and twigs
that it likes to eat. Desert Cottontails have
yellow-brown fur above and white fur below.

FOREFOOT:
SMALL, OVAL PRINTS

HIND FOOT:
LONG NARROW
PRINTS

The backs of their necks are orange. Their ears are longer
than those of other rabbits, with black tips. Like all rabbits
they are fast runners, but they can also swim and even
climb small trees. Females have up to five litters of two to four
young each and raise them in a fur-lined hollow in the ground.

Brush Rabbit

Sylvilagus bachmani LENGTH **11–15 in (28–38 cm)** · RANGE **West Coast,
Oregon through California** · HABITAT **Thick brush** · FOOD **Grasses, clover, berries**
· ACTIVE ⬤ ⬤

HIND FOOT:
LONG NARROW
PRINTS

FOREFOOT:
SMALL, OVAL
PRINTS

> → **LISTEN FOR THIS** When
> faced with danger, a rabbit may
> send out an alarm signal by thump-
> ing its hind foot on the ground and
> squealing loudly.

These small western rabbits like to stay
hidden in grass and shrubs during the day,
but they will come out in the morning and
evening to eat. You might see where they
have made paths through the grass between
their sleeping and feeding spots. Brush
Rabbits have grayish brown fur, short legs
and ears, and small fluffy "cottontails," dark
on top and white underneath. Females
have up to four litters a year of two to five
young, which they raise in soft nests. One
subspecies of Brush Rabbit in California's
San Joaquin Valley is endangered.

Eastern Cottontail

Sylvilagus floridanus LENGTH 15–18 in (38–46 cm) · RANGE Canada, eastern and central U.S. · HABITAT Brushy areas, fields, prairies, lawns · FOOD Grasses, clover, green plants, twigs · ACTIVE N L

This rabbit, with its powder puff white tail, is a common sight in much of the U.S. It lives in a wide range of brushy places, but particularly in areas where hedges or trees give way to open grass. Eastern Cottontails are grizzled brownish gray on top and pale below. Orange fur marks the back of their necks. Their ears are long and their tails are short, fluffy, and white on the underside. They eat a wide range of grasses and plants, including vegetables and flowers, much to the annoyance of gardeners. In breeding season, which is late winter through summer, males and females will dance and jump around each other. Cottontails give birth to lots of babies. From late winter until fall, females have up to seven litters of one to nine young each.

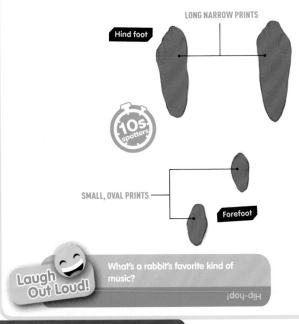

LONG NARROW PRINTS

Hind foot

SMALL, OVAL PRINTS

Forefoot

Laugh Out Loud!

What's a rabbit's favorite kind of music?

Hip-hop!

Mountain Cottontail

Sylvilagus nuttallii LENGTH 14–15 in (35.5–38 cm) · RANGE Canada, western U.S. · HABITAT Rocky areas, woods, desert brush · FOOD Grasses, sagebrush, juniper berries · ACTIVE Ⓝ Ⓛ

Living in dry, rocky areas, the shy Mountain Cottontail spends much of its time looking for food. It is a medium-size rabbit with grizzled tan fur above and a white belly. Its ears are relatively short, black-tipped, and furry. Its hind legs are covered with thick fur. In spring and summer, females give birth to up to five litters of three to eight young. They raise them in a cup-shaped nest lined with fur and covered over with leaves.

HIND FOOT: LONG NARROW PRINTS

FOREFOOT: SMALL, OVAL PRINTS

EXPERT'S CIRCLE

DON'T BE FOOLED To tell the **Mountain Cottontail** and **Desert Cottontail** (page 83) apart, look at the ears. Desert Cottontail ears don't have black tips and don't have much fur. Mountain Cottontail ears are black-tipped and furry.

Marsh Rabbit

Sylvilagus palustris LENGTH 14–18 in (35.5–46 cm) · RANGE Coastal southeastern U.S. · HABITAT Marshes, swamps, lake edges · FOOD Green plants, roots, twigs · ACTIVE Ⓝ Ⓛ

When in danger, Marsh Rabbits head for the water. These fine swimmers even lurk just under the water with only their eyes and nose showing, watching for predators. These small rabbits have reddish brown fur on top and white bellies. Their ears and tail are small, and unlike other cottontails, their tails are brownish gray. Marsh Rabbits often walk on all fours like a dog and can stand up and walk on their hind legs as well. Among thick marsh plants they build grassy, fur-lined nests and give birth to several litters a year of two to five young apiece.

HIND FOOT: LONG NARROW PRINTS

FOREFOOT: SMALL, OVAL PRINTS

Be an ANIMAL ACE!

One subspecies of Marsh Rabbit, the Lower Keys Rabbit, is endangered. These small bunnies live only on islands near South Florida.

Lesser Long-nosed Bat

Leptonycteris yerbabuenae LENGTH 3 in (7.5 cm) • RANGE
Southern Arizona, southwestern New Mexico • HABITAT Deserts, caves
• FOOD Desert flower nectar and pollen, cactus fruit • ACTIVE 🌙 🌍

Living only in the deserts of the deep Southwest, these bats love flowers. At night they fly out from the caves and mines where they rest during the day. When they find a cactus or agave in bloom, they stick their long tongues into the flowers to pick up nectar or pollen to eat. When flowering season is over, they eat fruit. Lesser Long-Nosed Bats are small and reddish brown, with tiny tails. They have long snouts with a little leaflike flap on the tip, much like the California Leaf-nosed Bat. Like many bats, they live in large colonies. In breeding season, these bats migrate into the United States from Mexico. Females live in a separate maternity colony with thousands of bats. There they give birth to one pup each year before returning to Mexico in the fall. Lesser Long-Nosed Bats are endangered in the United States.

Be an ANIMAL ACE!

Bats belong to the order Chiroptera. They are common and widespread around the world, although some species are endangered. They are the only mammals that truly fly. All bats are nocturnal, or active at night. Most eat insects, but some dine on flower nectar, pollen, fruit, frogs, fish, and blood.

BROAD WING

FOREARM 2 IN (5 CM)

TOTAL WINGSPAN 10 IN (25.5 CM)

10s. spotters

California Leaf-nosed Bat

Macrotus californicus LENGTH 3–4 in (7.5–10.2 cm) • RANGE **Southern California, Nevada, Arizona** • HABITAT **Deserts, mines** • FOOD **Flying insects, beetles, crickets** • ACTIVE **N L**

Darting about on its broad wings, the California Leaf-nosed Bat snaps up insects in the air and on the ground. These bats have noticeably big ears and eyes and large leaflike flaps on their noses. Their fur is gray or dark brown on top and pale underneath. They roost in small groups in caves or abandoned mines during the day. At night, they come out to hunt for about an hour before going back to their roosts. Females give birth to one to two young every June.

TOTAL WINGSPAN
13 IN (33 CM)

FOREARM
2 IN (5 CM)

It's a myth that bats are blind. Most, like the California Leaf-nosed Bat, have excellent vision.

Western Bonneted Bat

TOTAL WINGSPAN
1.8 FT (0.6 M)

FOREARM 3 IN
(7.5 CM)

Eumops perotis LENGTH 6–7.5 in (15–19 cm) • RANGE **Southern California, extreme Southwest** • HABITAT **Deserts, canyons** • FOOD **Moths, other flying insects, crickets, grasshoppers** • ACTIVE **N L**

With a wingspan almost two feet (0.6 m) across, this is the largest bat in North America. It's called a bonneted bat because its two big ears connect at their base and reach out across its forehead like a bonnet. Dark brown fur covers its body. Its wings are long and narrow and its tail is skinny. Also called the Western Mastiff Bat, this bat can't take off from the ground. Western Bonneted Bats roost in cracks in cliffs and launch themselves from on high, dropping a few feet before their wings pick up enough lift to fly. As they zoom about during the night, snatching up insects to eat, they squeak loudly. During the day, they rest in small colonies. The females give birth to one pup each year in early summer.

Brazilian Free-tailed Bat

Tadarida brasiliensis LENGTH 3.5–4 in (8.9–10.2 cm) • RANGE Southern U.S. from East to West Coasts • HABITAT Deserts, farms, canyons • FOOD Moths, other flying insects • ACTIVE ◐ ◑

If you are lucky enough to visit New Mexico's Carlsbad Caverns in the evening, you will see an awesome sight. With a roar of wings, millions upon millions of Brazilian Free-tailed Bats fly out of the caves, looking like a thick trail of smoke. They are in search of food for their young. Brazilian Free-tailed Bats are one of the most numerous mammals in the country, with up to 100 million living across the South. They roost in huge numbers in caves, migrating to Mexico in the winter and raising their young in the United States in the summer. These bats are small, with grayish brown fur, wide ears, and skinny tails. Flying on narrow, pointed wings they are super fast, reaching speeds of 60 miles an hour (96 km/h). Each night, they may travel for 50 miles (80 km) at heights up to 9,800 feet (3,000 m). Females raise one pup each year in closely packed colonies.

Be an ANIMAL ACE!

Even though the bat pups are squished together by the thousands, the mothers that have been out at night searching for food can find their own pup's special call and smell when they come home in the morning.

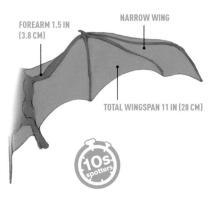

FOREARM 1.5 IN (3.8 CM)

NARROW WING

TOTAL WINGSPAN 11 IN (28 CM)

10s spotters

Big Brown Bat

Eptesicus fuscus LENGTH 4–5 in (10.2–12.7 cm)
• RANGE Canada, U.S. except South Florida and south-
central Texas • HABITAT Farms, cities, suburbs, parks,
woods • FOOD Beetles, other flying insects • ACTIVE 🌙 🌓

If you've ever seen a bat flitting
around in your house or school,
it might have been a Big Brown
Bat. These common, widespread
mammals like to roost in attics
and other high places in buildings.
Big Brown Bats are large, with shiny
brown fur and pale bellies. Their snouts, ears, wings, and tail are black.
Although they hibernate in winter, they may wake up and come out to
hunt on warmer days. Females give birth to one or two pups each year
in maternity colonies. Because they eat June bugs and other insect
pests, Big Brown Bats are especially helpful around farms.

FOREARM 2 IN (5 CM)   BROAD WING

TOTAL WINGSPAN 13 IN (33 CM)

Be an ANIMAL ACE!

Like many—but not all—bats,
Big Brown Bats use echolocation
to get around at night.
Echolocation is a way of seeing
with sound. The bats give off
very high pitched squeaks or
clicks through their mouths or
noses. The sounds bounce off
insects and objects and return to
the bats' ears. Putting these
echoes together gives the bat a
mental map of its surroundings.

Eastern Red Bat

Lasiurus borealis LENGTH 4–5 in (10.2–12.7 cm) · RANGE Canada, central and eastern U.S. · HABITAT Woods, fields, forest edges · FOOD Moths and other flying insects · ACTIVE Ⓝ Ⓛ

Dangling from a branch, this reddish brown bat looks like an autumn leaf, a kind of camouflage that may keep it hidden from its enemies. The males are distinctly red or orange and the females are a paler red. Both have frosted tips on their silky fur and white patches on their shoulders. Eastern Red Bats are shy forest mammals. During the day, they hang out in the trees. At night, they fly out to feast on moths, beetles, and other insects. In winter, they migrate south to hibernate. In spring, they fly north, where the females have two to four pups each summer. The mothers raise these pups in their roosts among the leaves.

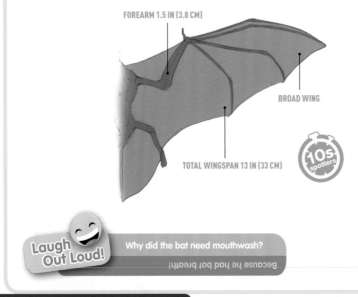

FOREARM 1.5 IN (3.8 CM)

BROAD WING

TOTAL WINGSPAN 13 IN (33 CM)

10s spotters

Laugh Out Loud!

Why did the bat need mouthwash?

Because he had bat breath!

Hoary Bat

Lasiurus cinereus LENGTH 4–6 in (10.2–15 cm) • RANGE Canada, entire U.S. • HABITAT Woods, canyons • FOOD Moths and other flying insects • ACTIVE 🌙 🌓

TOTAL WINGSPAN 17 IN (43 CM)

FOREARM 2 IN (5 CM)

These bats are long-distance travelers. Hoary Bats are found all over the lower 48 states, in Canada, and as far away as Hawaii and Iceland. Large with frosty brown fur, they have a yellow band of fur around their heads. During the day they roost by themselves in trees. At night they hunt, flying in quick straight paths across the sky. Males and females spend most of the year apart. In fall, they migrate south together, returning in spring. Females have one to four pups in early summer.

TOTAL WINGSPAN 15 IN (38 CM)

FOREARM 2 IN (5 CM)

Northern Yellow Bat

Lasiurus intermedius LENGTH 4.5 in (11.5 cm) • RANGE Southeastern coast • HABITAT Forests, palms, Spanish moss • FOOD Mosquitoes, flies, other flying insects • ACTIVE 🌙 🌓

A native of the Southeast, the Northern Yellow Bat likes to roost in trees with dangling clumps of Spanish moss. It's a handsome little mammal with silky yellow brown fur and pointed ears. Northern Yellow Bats live by themselves most of the time, but females with pups will gather in nursery colonies. In their warm climate, these bats don't need to migrate or hibernate. Females have two to four young in early summer.

DANGER! ☠

Bats, skunks, raccoons, foxes, and some other mammals can carry rabies, a dangerous disease. Always stay clear of any mammal that seems ill or is acting strangely. This particularly applies to any bats you might see on the ground. Never get close to them or pick them up! Ask an adult to call an animal control officer or the health department.

Seminole Bat

Lasiurus seminolus LENGTH 4 in (10.2 cm) · RANGE Southeastern U.S. · HABITAT Forests, swamps, Spanish moss · FOOD Flies, beetles, other flying insects · ACTIVE 🌙 🌘

Like Northern Yellow Bats, Seminole Bats like to roost in trees with hanging Spanish moss. They are also known as Mahogany Bats because of their rich red-brown fur, the color of mahogany wood. Their fur has frosty tips, and their throats and chests have white patches. Their ears are short and round. In the evening, Seminole Bats drop out of their roosts and zoom about hunting flying insects, often snatching them up around streetlights. They don't hibernate, but they do move south in winter and north in summer. Females have three to four young in early summer.

Bat wings evolved from the arm and hand bones of early mammals. Try drawing your own, using your own hands. You'll need:

- Construction or other thick paper
- Crayons
- Safe scissors
- Tape

1. Press one hand down on one half of the paper, spread your fingers, and trace around the hand with the crayon. On the other half, do the same with the other hand.
2. Draw a curved line from fingertip to fingertip.
3. Carefully cut out each webbed hand.
4. Tape the two hand-wings together at the bottom of the thumbs for your own pair of bat wings.

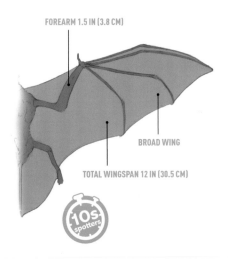

FOREARM 1.5 IN (3.8 CM)

BROAD WING

TOTAL WINGSPAN 12 IN (30.5 CM)

10s spotters

Pallid Bat

Antrozous pallidus LENGTH 4–5 in (10.2–12.7 cm) •
RANGE Washington State into Southwest • HABITAT Deserts,
canyons • FOOD Ground insects • ACTIVE ◐ ●

Unlike other bats, the Pallid
Bat likes its food on the
ground. Using its big ears to
hear scurrying prey, it swoops
down out of the night to pick
off crickets, beetles, and even
scorpions and lizards. The term
"pallid" means "pale." Pallid Bats
are large, with pale, sand-colored
fur on top and white fur below. They
have huge ears, big eyes, and doglike snouts.
They are social bats, living in colonies in caves, mines, hollow
trees, or buildings. During the day, they rest in one roost, then
at night they move to another one where they can maintain
their daytime body heat. Females give birth to one to three
young in early summer.

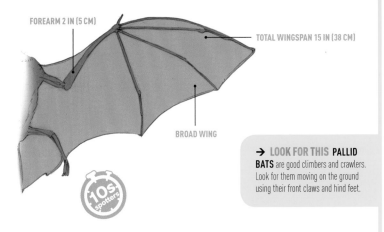

FOREARM 2 IN (5 CM)

TOTAL WINGSPAN 15 IN (38 CM)

BROAD WING

10s
spotters

→ **LOOK FOR THIS PALLID
BATS** are good climbers and crawlers.
Look for them moving on the ground
using their front claws and hind feet.

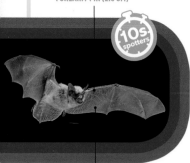

FOREARM 1 IN (2.5 CM)

TOTAL WINGSPAN 7.5 IN (19 CM)

Western Pipistrelle

Pipistrellus hesperus LENGTH 2–3.5 in (5–8.9 cm) • RANGE Washington State into Southwest • HABITAT Deserts, canyons, grassy areas • FOOD Small flying insects • ACTIVE 🌑 🌓

Fluttering slowly through the desert sky, these tiny bats can look like butterflies. Western Pipistrelles are the smallest bats in the United States. Only two or three inches (5–7.5 cm) long, the adults weigh as much as a penny. The pups weigh less than a paperclip. Western Pipistrelles have yellowish fur above and whitish bellies. Their wings, ears, nose and feet are black. They roost in caves, mines, and buildings near water, and they come out in the evening and morning to hunt flying insects. To drink, they zoom across the water's surface and sip the water while in flight. Despite their small size, females manage to give birth to twin pups in maternity colonies each June.

Eastern Pipistrelle

Pipistrellus subflavus LENGTH 3–3.5 in (7.5–8.9 cm) • RANGE Eastern half of U.S. • HABITAT Woods, farms • FOOD Small flying insects • ACTIVE 🌑 🌓

FOREARM 1 IN (2.5 CM)

Like its western cousin, the Eastern Pipistrelle is a tiny bat. About three inches (7.5 cm) long, it has reddish brown fur. The hairs have three distinct colors: dark at the bottom, light in the middle, and dark at the top. Their faces and forearms are pinkish brown.

In summer, Eastern Pipistrelles roost in hollow trees or buildings. During that time, females have twin pups in small maternity colonies. Males live alone. In winter, both males and females migrate south and hibernate together in caves or abandoned mines.

TOTAL WINGSPAN 9 IN (23 CM)

NAME GAME

The "Vesper" in these bats' family name means "evening." Most vesper bats come out to eat around dusk.

Rafinesque's Big-eared Bat

Corynorhinus rafinesquii LENGTH 3.5–4 in (8.9–10.2 cm)
• RANGE Southeastern U.S. • HABITAT Forests • FOOD Moths, other flying insects • ACTIVE 🌙 🌓

"Big-eared bat" is right: This bat's huge ears are bigger than its head. When it's not using them to listen for prey, it folds them back. Rafinesque's Big-eared Bats have brown fur on their backs and paler fur on their bellies. Their noses are topped by two fleshy lumps. They are excellent fliers and can hover in the air like a bee. In winter, they hibernate in colonies, sometimes sharing their shelters with other kinds of bats. In early summer, females give birth to one pup in a small maternity colony. The bats roost together in summer and will groom each other while they hang from their perches.

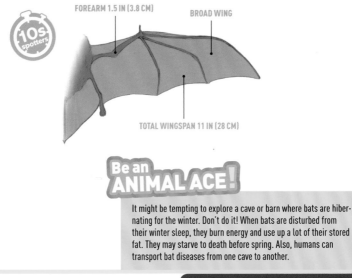

10s spotters

FOREARM 1.5 IN (3.8 CM)

BROAD WING

TOTAL WINGSPAN 11 IN (28 CM)

Be an ANIMAL ACE!

It might be tempting to explore a cave or barn where bats are hibernating for the winter. Don't do it! When bats are disturbed from their winter sleep, they burn energy and use up a lot of their stored fat. They may starve to death before spring. Also, humans can transport bat diseases from one cave to another.

MAMMAL MANIA: ENDANGERED!

GRIZZLY BEARS ARE THREATENED AND MAY SOON BECOME ENDANGERED.

Once, Gray Wolves and Grizzly Bears lived throughout northern North America. Black-footed Ferrets lived side by side with prairie dogs. Today, these mammals and more have been wiped out from large parts of their earlier ranges. There are many reasons for this. Habitat loss is one. People have been replacing forests, grasslands, and swamps with farms, houses, and roads. Pollution, climate change, new diseases, and hunting have also played a part. Today, species in danger of becoming extinct are listed by the government as endangered or threatened. Some, with human intervention, are recovering. Others remain in serious trouble.

Fighting for Ferrets

The sleek little Black-footed Ferret (page 117), a native of the American prairies, was once believed to be extinct. These ferrets depended upon prairie dogs as their main food, and they also took over prairie dog burrows for their homes. As humans wiped out the prairie dog's habitat, they wiped out almost all Black-footed Ferrets as well. When a few were discovered still alive in the 1980s, scientists captured 18 of them and began breeding them in captivity. Today, over a thousand are back living in the wild. They are still endangered, but the effort to save this species continues.

Battling for Bats

In winter, Indiana Bats hibernate by the tens of thousands in central U.S. caves. So how can they be endangered? The problem is that they group together in very few caves and can die if they're disturbed while they're hibernating. They are also dying from white-nose syndrome, a new disease carried by a fungus. These threats have cut their population in half in the last 10 years. Their roosts and caves are being protected, and scientists are working on a cure for white-nose syndrome, which affects other bat species, too.

Working for Wolves

In the 1700s, about two million Gray Wolves (page 107) lived across most of the United States. Human settlers were afraid the wolves would eat farm animals—and farmers—so they hunted and trapped the wolves and destroyed their wild lands. By the 1960s, Gray Wolves had mostly vanished from the lower 48 states, although many remained in Alaska. With government protection in the 1970s and relocation to Yellowstone National Park and Idaho in the 1990s, they began making a comeback. They are still endangered in 46 states, and conservationists continue their work.

TOTAL WINGSPAN 11.5 IN (29 CM)

Silver-haired Bat

Lasionycteris noctivagans LENGTH 3.5–4 in (8.9–10.2 cm) ▪ RANGE Canada, most of U.S. except far South ▪ HABITAT Forests ▪ FOOD Moths, other flying insects ▪ ACTIVE **N** **L**

The Silver-haired Bat makes its home in forests across much of the United States. In summer, these bats roost during the day under loose tree bark or in holes in dead trees. In the evening and before dawn, they come out to fly slowly about in search of moths and other flying insects to eat. Silver-haired Bats have dark brown or black fur with silvery tips. Their faces are dark and their ears are small and round. Males and females live apart during the summer. In winter, they migrate south. In early summer, females give birth to two pups.

FOREARM 1.5 IN (3.8 CM)

10s. spotters

TOTAL WINGSPAN 10 IN (25.5 CM)

Long-eared Myotis

Myotis evotis LENGTH 3–4 in (7.5–10.2 cm) ▪ RANGE Canada, western U.S. except extreme Southwest ▪ HABITAT Forests, grasslands ▪ FOOD Moths, other flying insects ▪ ACTIVE **N** **L**

These fluffy western bats fly out to hunt in the cool early night. At times, they will turn off their echolocation and catch an insect using their hearing alone. Long-eared Myotis are small, with large dark ears. Their light to dark brown fur is long and shiny. They typically roost in dead trees, resting during the day as the sun warms the wood. Males and females live separately. In summer, females join together in small maternity colonies, where they bear one pup each.

FOREARM 1.5 IN (3.8 CM)

10s. spotters

Be an ANIMAL ACE!

Bats are great at insect control. A single bat can eat thousands of moths, mosquitoes, and other insects in a night. Just one cave in Texas—Bracken Cave—has a bat colony that eats 250 tons (227 t) of insects each night in the summer.

Little Brown Myotis

Myotis lucifugus **LENGTH 3–3.5 in (7.5–8.9 cm) · RANGE Canada, U.S. except southwestern and south-central states · HABITAT Forests near water · FOOD Water insects, moths, mosquitoes · ACTIVE N L**

This little mammal, also known as the Little Brown Bat, lives across much of the United States. It often roosts in buildings during the day, flying out at night over the water, looking for swarms of insects. At night, these bats return to different roosts, collecting in large colonies. Little Brown Myotis have shiny brown fur above and paler bellies. Their ears are small and their hind feet are big. In the winter, they migrate to warmer areas and hibernate, returning in the spring to give birth to one pup each in maternity colonies. Unlike many other small mammals, bats can live a long time. Little Brown Myotis are a good example, with some living up to 30 years in the wild.

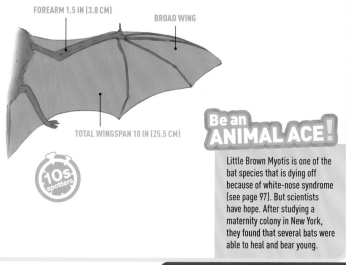

FOREARM 1.5 IN (3.8 CM)

BROAD WING

TOTAL WINGSPAN 10 IN (25.5 CM)

10s spotters

Be an ANIMAL ACE!

Little Brown Myotis is one of the bat species that is dying off because of white-nose syndrome (see page 97). But scientists have hope. After studying a maternity colony in New York, they found that several bats were able to heal and bear young.

Ocelot

Leopardus pardalis LENGTH 3–4.5 ft (0.9–1.4 m) • RANGE Extreme southern Texas and Arizona • HABITAT Forests, brushy areas • FOOD Rodents, other small mammals, birds, reptiles, fish, frogs • ACTIVE 🌙 🌆

The Ocelot is a shy and beautiful cat. It is rarely seen in the United States, living only on the far southern borders of Texas and Arizona. This medium-size cat has gorgeous fur: Its black-ringed brown spots and bars stand out against a gray or tan background. Its tail is long and paws are big. Ocelots come out mostly at night and in the evenings. Like all cats, they are excellent hunters and devoted meat-eaters, tracking down small mammals, birds, fish, frogs, and even lizards. They climb and swim well. Females have one to three kittens every two years or so in the fall and winter. Because so much of their habitat has been destroyed, and because hunters have killed them for their lovely fur, Ocelots are now endangered in the United States. It is illegal to kill or capture them or to sell their skins.

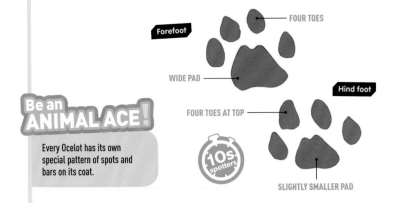

FOUR TOES

Forefoot

WIDE PAD

Hind foot

FOUR TOES AT TOP

SLIGHTLY SMALLER PAD

Be an ANIMAL ACE!

Every Ocelot has its own special pattern of spots and bars on its coat.

10s spotters

Canada Lynx

Lynx canadensis **LENGTH 2.5–3.5 ft (0.8–1 m)**
RANGE Alaska, Northwest U.S., Rocky Mountains, northern Northeast, Canada • HABITAT Deep forests • FOOD Snowshoe Hares, rodents, birds, deer • ACTIVE 🌙 🕐

Creeping quietly through the snow on its big, furry paws, the Canada Lynx is a deadly hunter of the far north. Because its main prey is the Snowshoe Hare (page 80), the Canada Lynx numbers rise and fall as the number of hares rises and falls from year to year. When they have more meat than they can eat at once, the lynx may store it under snow or leaves to eat later. Canada Lynx are medium-size cats with thick, grayish tan fur and short tails. Their ears are topped by long black tufts, and long fur hangs down from the sides of their faces like droopy sideburns. Like most cats, they keep to themselves for most of the year. Females have one to six kittens once a year in the spring. Canada Lynx have been overhunted for their fur, and for that reason the species is listed as threatened in the United States.

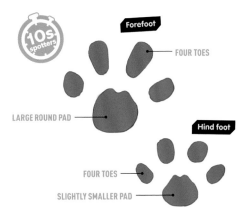

Forefoot
FOUR TOES
LARGE ROUND PAD

Hind foot
FOUR TOES
SLIGHTLY SMALLER PAD

Bobcat

Lynx rufus LENGTH 2–4 ft (0.6–1.2 m) · RANGE Canada, across U.S.
except upper Midwest · HABITAT Forests, swamps, rocky dry areas
FOOD Rabbits, wide variety of mammals, birds · ACTIVE 🌙 🌆

This adaptable wildcat can be found in most of the country, from the swamps of Florida to the forests of Washington State. You won't often see it, though: It is a lone nighttime hunter and stays away from humans. Bobcats are stocky and furry, about twice the size of house cats. Their coats are brownish or grayish on top and white below, with blurry spots on the sides and black bars on the legs. Their ears have a small black tuft and their tails are short and stubby, with a tip that's black on top and white below. Bobcats trail their prey along well-worn hunting paths and will eat a wide range of mammals from rabbits and mice to opossums. Females have one litter of one to six kittens per year in the spring.

EXPERT'S CIRCLE

DON'T BE FOOLED
Bobcat and **Canada Lynx** (page 101) ranges overlap in the upper United States/lower Canada region and the animals can be hard to tell apart. Bobcats have shorter legs, smaller ear tufts, and tails that are white on the bottom.

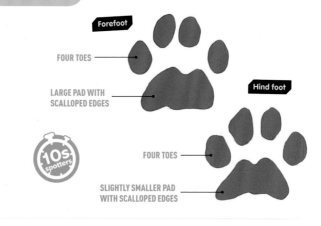

Forefoot
FOUR TOES
LARGE PAD WITH SCALLOPED EDGES

Hind foot
FOUR TOES
SLIGHTLY SMALLER PAD WITH SCALLOPED EDGES

10s spotters

Mountain Lion

Puma concolor LENGTH 5–8 ft (1.5–2.4 m) · RANGE
Canada, western U.S., southern Florida · HABITAT Dry
mountains, deserts, forests · FOOD Deer, other large and
medium-size mammals · ACTIVE 🌐 🌙

The Mountain Lion—also known
as Cougar, Puma, Panther, or
Catamount—is the largest wildcat
in North America. Strong and
lightning-fast, it can run up to 50 miles
an hour (80 km/h) for short distances and
jump more than 20 feet (6 m). Mountain Lions hunt
deer and other mammals in remote areas, stalking their prey silently
before leaping onto the animal's back and biting it. If Mountain Lions have
too much to eat at once, they will store the remains under leaves and
sticks. These top predators are long and sleek. Their short fur is pale
brown to reddish above and pale below.
Their ears are short and round and their
long tails have a black tip. Every other
year, a female will give birth to a litter of
one to six cubs. One subspecies, the
Florida Panther, is critically endangered,
with about 230 remaining in the wild.

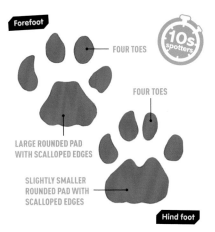

Forefoot

FOUR TOES

FOUR TOES

10s spotters

LARGE ROUNDED PAD
WITH SCALLOPED EDGES

SLIGHTLY SMALLER
ROUNDED PAD WITH
SCALLOPED EDGES

Hind foot

DANGER! ☠️

On rare occasions, a
Mountain Lion will attack a
human. When you're out in
Mountain Lion territory, follow certain safety rules:

• Don't hike or bike alone.
  Don't straggle behind
  your group.

• Be careful when crouching
  down or bending:
  Mountain Lions are more
  likely to attack then.

• If you see one, don't
  approach it and don't run.
  They like to chase and are
  faster than you are.

• If threatened, make yourself look big and back
  away slowly.

Arctic Fox

HIND FOOT:
FOUR ROUNDED TOES;
WITH CLAWS

Vulpes lagopus LENGTH 2.5–3 ft (0.8–0.9 m) • RANGE Alaska, Canada • HABITAT Tundra, ice floes • FOOD Rodents, hares, fish, birds, eggs, carrion • ACTIVE N L

When winter arrives, the thick coat of the Arctic Fox changes from grayish brown to snowy white. Some turn a bluish gray color in winter. With this warm fur, short legs and ears, and furry feet, this compact member of the canine family is well adapted to its frigid home in the far north. These bold animals eat almost anything, from small mammals to fish and eggs. In winter, they often follow Polar Bears or wolves to snack on their leftovers. Arctic Foxes mate for life, with a male and female together raising two litters of one to five kits a year.

FOREFOOT:
FOUR ROUNDED TOES;
WITH CLAWS

Swift Fox

HIND FOOT:
SMALL PAD;
FOUR TOES WITH CLAWS

Vulpes velox LENGTH 2–2.6 ft (0.6–0.8 m) • RANGE Canada, High Plains from Texas into Idaho • HABITAT Grasslands, desert • FOOD Rodents, other mammals, birds, lizards, insects, plants • ACTIVE N L

This little fox is as fast as its name. Dashing after prey or escaping from an enemy, it can run as fast as 25 miles an hour (40 km/h). Swift Foxes have grayish yellow fur on top, orangish sides, and pale bellies. Their ears are large and pointed and tails have a black tip. They eat almost anything, from mice to berries. Males and females mate for life and live in underground dens, where they have one litter each year of two to six young. If the female dies, the male raises the kits by himself until they are old enough to leave home.

FOREFOOT:
SMALL PAD;
FOUR TOES WITH CLAWS

Be an
ANIMAL ACE!

The Swift Fox almost became extinct in the 1930s. Traps and poison set out for wolves and Coyotes also killed these little foxes in large numbers. They were successfully brought back in the 1970s, but they live in only part of their former range.

Red Fox

Vulpes vulpes LENGTH **3–3.5 ft (0.9–1 m)** ▪ RANGE
Canada, most of U.S. except parts of West and Southwest
▪ HABITAT **Fields, woods, brushlands, suburbs, cities**
▪ FOOD **Mammals, birds, insects, plants** ▪ ACTIVE 🌙 🌓

The Red Fox will eat almost anything, but it has a special move
to catch mice under the snow.
After standing still and listening for tiny hidden movements,
it leaps high into the air and
dives headfirst into the snow.
It doesn't always succeed, but often
it comes up with a mouse twitching in its jaws. Moves like these
are among the skills that make Red Foxes such widespread and
adaptable mammals. They are the largest U.S. foxes, with orangish
red fur on their backs, pale fur on their bellies, and long bushy
tails with white tips. Their ears are big and pointed. They live in
dens, sometimes borrowing those dug by Woodchucks or badgers.
Males and females often mate for life. Together they raise one
litter of one to nine pups each year.

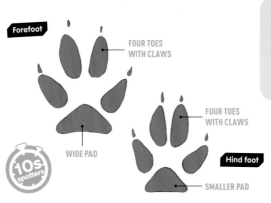

Forefoot
FOUR TOES
WITH CLAWS
WIDE PAD

FOUR TOES
WITH CLAWS
Hind foot
SMALLER PAD

10s spotters

→ LISTEN FOR THIS
RED FOXES are often out at
night on suburban or even city
streets. Listen for the high-
pitched, screaming bark of the
female (called a vixen) as she
calls to her pups.

Common Gray Fox

HIND FOOT: PAD NARROWER THAN FOREFOOT; FOUR LARGE TOES WITH CLAWS

Urocyon cinereoargenteus LENGTH 2.5–3.5 ft (0.8–1 m) · RANGE Canada, most of U.S. except upper Northwest · HABITAT Woods, brush · FOOD Mammals, lizards, frogs, insects, fruit, nuts · ACTIVE 🌙 🌓

Searching for a Common Gray Fox? Look up! Common Grays are the only members of the dog family that can climb trees. There, they hide from their enemies or just relax on a branch. Grays have grizzled gray fur on top of their bodies and reddish fur on their ears, neck, and sides. Their chests are white or tan. They aren't picky eaters, chowing down on almost anything, from rabbits to fruit. In spring, they give birth to an average of four pups, which can take care of themselves by about seven months of age.

FOREFOOT: SMALL TRIANGULAR PAD; FOUR LARGE TOES WITH CLAWS

EXPERT'S CIRCLE

DON'T BE FOOLED
Common Gray and **Red Foxes** (page 105) share much of the same range. Grays are grayer on top and don't have a white tip on their tails.

Coyote

FOREFOOT: SMALL TRIANGULAR FOOT PAD; FOUR LARGE TOES WITH CLAWS

Canis latrans LENGTH 3.5–4 ft (1–1.3 m) · RANGE Alaska, west and south Canada, all of U.S. · HABITAT Open dry areas in West, brushy areas in East, suburbs, cities · FOOD Mammals, birds, snakes, insects, carrion, plants · ACTIVE 🌞 🌓

One of the most adaptable mammals in North America, the coyote lives in deserts, grasslands, cities, and suburbs. It eats almost anything and has few enemies aside from humans. Coyotes are members of the dog family, with pointed, triangular faces, bushy tails, and skinny legs. Their fur is grizzled, orange gray above and pale below, and their tails have a black tip. Eastern coyotes, whose ancestors may have bred with gray wolves, are larger than western ones. People may hear coyotes at night near their neighborhood. Their varied calls include barks, howls, and sharp yips. Coyotes live either by themselves, in pairs, or in family groups. They have one litter of cubs every spring.

HIND FOOT: PAD SLIGHTLY NARROWER THAN FOREFOOT; FOUR LARGE TOES WITH CLAWS

Gray Wolf

Canis lupus **LENGTH 4–6 ft (1.2–1.8 m)** ● **RANGE Canada, Alaska, north-central U.S., Northwest** ● **HABITAT Forests, tundra** ● **FOOD Moose, elk, other mammals** ● **ACTIVE** ⬤ ⬤ ⬤ ⬤

The magnificent Gray Wolf is the largest wild canine in the world. It usually has grizzled gray fur, but it can come in colors from white to black. Its legs are long and its tail is long and bushy, with a black tip. Very social animals, Gray Wolves live in family packs that are led by a mated pair, known as the alpha male and alpha female. Sometimes an unrelated lone wolf will join a pack. Gray Wolves are top predators that chase down large animals such as moose or elk, but they will eat little mammals when they need to. Their packs travel through large territories, covering up to 260 square miles (675 sq km). Only the alpha male and female will breed, producing a litter of 1 to 11 pups each spring. The whole pack pitches in to raise the youngsters.

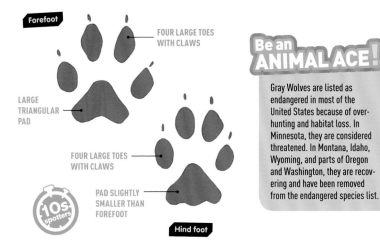

Forefoot

FOUR LARGE TOES WITH CLAWS

LARGE TRIANGULAR PAD

FOUR LARGE TOES WITH CLAWS

PAD SLIGHTLY SMALLER THAN FOREFOOT

Hind foot

Be an ANIMAL ACE!

Gray Wolves are listed as endangered in most of the United States because of over-hunting and habitat loss. In Minnesota, they are considered threatened. In Montana, Idaho, Wyoming, and parts of Oregon and Washington, they are recovering and have been removed from the endangered species list.

MAMMAL MANIA:
MAMMALS IN THE HOUSE

DOMESTIC SHORT-HAIRED CATS HAVE MIXED ANCESTRY, AND THEIR COATS CAN BE A RANGE OF COLORS.

Many of us live side by side with mammals in our own homes. Dogs and cats have been human companions for thousands of years. This seems like a long time, but in scientific terms it's practically yesterday: These animals are still the same species as their wild ancestors. They have evolved into different shapes, sizes, and colors, but they can still breed with their wild cousins. Exactly why and when these animals became our household pets is still unknown. Research suggests that it was as much their idea as our own.

Wolves to Dogs

All pet dogs, from Chihuahuas to Golden Retrievers, evolved from early wolves. This likely started between 20,000 and 40,000 years ago, when humans lived in small tribes as hunters and gatherers. We don't know why the first hunter took the first wolf into his home. He might have captured a mild-mannered wolf to breed into a hunting companion, protector, or buddy. Over time, wolves developed the look of modern dogs—with the help of breeding by humans. Their ears became floppy, their coats grew spots, and their tails wagged. With these changes came changes to behavior. Dogs got friendlier and more aware of human gestures and feelings. They became the loving animals we know today.

Staying Wild

Cats and dogs became household pets thousands of years ago. Today, we know that it's a bad idea to try to make a pet out of a wild animal. Take good care of your beloved cat or dog, but let exotic animals live in the wild.

Wildcats to Cats

Household cats are all descended from small wildcats that lived (and still live) in the Middle East and Europe. Around 8,000 years ago, as people began farming and building cities, cats moved in with them. They probably hunted pestering rats and mice. By the days of ancient Egypt, cats had become companions. The Egyptian goddess Bastet is shown with a cat head in wall paintings, and some Egyptians mummified their cats after they died, like this one. When sailors took cats onto their boats to control mice and rats, cats started to spread around the world. Cats today have more spots and stripes, but they still look much like wildcats—and they are the same species.

Red Wolf

Canis rufus **LENGTH** 4–5 ft (1.2–1.5 m) • **RANGE** Reintroduced to North Carolina, South Carolina, Tennessee • **HABITAT** Forests, coastal plains, swamps • **FOOD** Raccoons, deer, other mammals • **ACTIVE** N E

The rare and endangered Red Wolf is a slimmer, sleeker version of its Gray Wolf relative. It is not particularly red, but it has short gray to red-brown fur on its back and a white belly. Its legs are slender and its head is narrow. Red Wolves once roamed the Southeast, but they were almost wiped out owing to habitat loss and hunting. In the 1970s, scientists captured some of the last Red Wolves and began to breed them in captivity. Small groups now live in the wild in the Southeast, in family packs led by a male and female pair. Members of the pack help the pair raise one litter of three to six pups each year.

FOREFOOT:
TRIANGULAR PAD;
FOUR TOES WITH CLAWS

HIND FOOT:
LONG PAD LIKE A HUMAN PRINT;
FIVE TOES WITH CLAWS

American Black Bear

Ursus americanus **LENGTH** 4–6 ft (1.2–1.8 m) • **RANGE** Canada, Alaska, western and northeastern U.S., isolated groups elsewhere • **HABITAT** Forests, swamps, mountains • **FOOD** Plants, berries, nuts, insects • **ACTIVE** B L

The adaptable American Black Bear mainly lives in forests, but it will also seek out food in campgrounds and back-yards. Big and burly, the males can weigh up to 600 pounds (270 kg). In the East, American Black Bears have black fur and lighter snouts. In the West, they can also be pale brown. A rare version called the Ghost, or Spirit, Bear lives in Canada and is white. American Black Bears are swift runners, good tree climbers, and fine swimmers. They eat leaves, berries, fruit, insects, small mammals, and even garbage and birdseed. In winter in most areas, they enter a deep sleep in their dens, coming out hungry in the spring. Every other year, females have one to five cubs.

FOREFOOT:
BROAD FRONT
PAD, SMALL
HIND PAD;
FIVE TOES
WITH CLAWS

> → **LOOK FOR THIS**
> Are these bears in your woods? Check trees for long claw slashes above head height, or tufts of fur from bears scratching against the bark.

Grizzly Bear

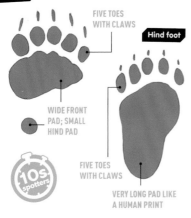

Ursus arctos **LENGTH 5.5–8.5 ft (1.7–2.6 m)** · **RANGE Canada, Alaska, northwestern U.S.** · **HABITAT Forests, open areas in mountains, rivers, coasts** · **FOOD Plants, berries, nuts, fish, mammals** · **ACTIVE** ⬤ ⬤ ⬤

The powerful Grizzly Bear is one of the planet's most impressive mammals. A male can weigh 900 pounds (410 kg) and stand nine feet tall (2.7 m) on its hind legs. These bears are called "grizzly" because some have grizzled brown fur, meaning their fur is streaked with a gray color. Others have plain tan, gray, reddish, or brown fur. Their bodies are thick, with a hump above the shoulders. Their eyes are small, ears are rounded, and claws are long and curved. Grizzlies usually move in a slow, lumbering walk and aren't good tree climbers, but they can run quickly. In winter, Grizzlies sleep in dens, coming out in the spring. Females have two or three cubs every two to four years. Grizzly Bears are listed as threatened in the lower 48 states, except in and around Yellowstone National Park.

DANGER!

Most Grizzlies will run from humans—but they are unpredictable and will sometimes attack, especially when guarding cubs. In Grizzly territory, stay alert and follow safety rules, including the following:

- Keep your distance: Watch bears from at least 100 yards (91 m) away.
- Stay in a group.
- Talk while hiking, so a bear knows you're a human.
- Never get between a mother bear and a cub.
- Learn proper storage rules for food: Don't keep it in your tent, backpack, or campsite.
- If face to face with a bear, don't run. Talk calmly, make yourself look big, and move away slowly and sideways.

Forefoot

FIVE TOES WITH CLAWS

Hind foot

WIDE FRONT PAD; SMALL HIND PAD

10s spotters

FIVE TOES WITH CLAWS

VERY LONG PAD LIKE A HUMAN PRINT

Northern River Otter

Lontra canadensis LENGTH 3–4.3 ft (0.9–1.3 m) • RANGE Canada, Alaska, north-western and eastern U.S. • HABITAT Streams, rivers, lakes, swamps, coasts • FOOD Fish, crayfish, frogs, small mammals, insects • ACTIVE ☼ ☾

Northern River Otters love to play. By themselves or in a group, these lively mammals delight in rolling around, sliding down riverbanks on their bellies, and surfing on waves. Their long, slender bodies twist and turn with grace. Otters are well designed for a watery life. They have sleek, short, dark brown fur above and silvery fur on their bellies. Their muscular tails, thick at the base and thinner toward the end, propel them through the water. The Combination of oil in their hair, webbed toes, and small ears also helps them speed along. They can stay underwater for several minutes, but they are also good runners on land. Once a year, females give birth to one to six young in a den near the water. Although otters are not endangered, hunting, trapping, and polluted waters have killed many of them. They are rarer than they used to be.

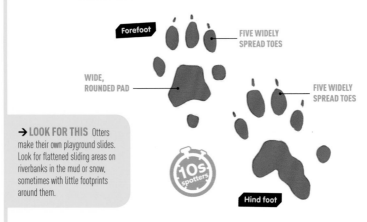

Forefoot

FIVE WIDELY SPREAD TOES

WIDE, ROUNDED PAD

FIVE WIDELY SPREAD TOES

→ LOOK FOR THIS Otters make their own playground slides. Look for flattened sliding areas on riverbanks in the mud or snow, sometimes with little footprints around them.

10s spotters

Hind foot

Wolverine

Gulo gulo LENGTH 2.6–3.6 ft (0.8–1.1 m) • RANGE Canada, Alaska, northern Rocky Mountains, some spots in West • HABITAT Northern forests, tundra, mountains • FOOD Large and small mammals, birds, eggs • ACTIVE 🌞 🌙

Strong and fierce, this member of the weasel family looks more like a little bear. It is stocky, or sturdy, with thick legs, a large head, and small round ears. Its fur is dark brown, and broad yellowish stripes run from its head to it rump. Wolverines live in small family groups in remote areas of northern forests. They seem to be always hungry, and will eat mammals many times their own size, such as Moose. Running swiftly on their broad paws, they catch the bigger animals that might have trouble escaping in thick snow. Wolverines boldly drive away big predators such as Mountain Lions or bears to steal their kills. Like other weasels, they have scent glands on their rumps and will mark their food caches with stinky spray to keep away other animals. Females have one litter of one to five young every other summer.

Forefoot

FOUR OR FIVE TOES

FOUR OR FIVE TOES

WIDE, ROUNDED PAD

10s spotters

Hind foot

WIDE PAD

Be an ANIMAL ACE!

How strong are Wolverine jaws? Airport officials in Newark, New Jersey, found out when a Wolverine being sent from Norway to Alaska chewed right through his metal cage. Luckily, the growling animal, named Kasper, didn't escape.

NAME GAME

The Wolverine's scientific name, *Gulo gulo*, means "glutton glutton."

American Marten

Martes americana LENGTH 1.6–2.3 ft (0.5–0.7 m) ◦ RANGE Alaska, northern
Rocky Mountains, some spots in West and Northeast, Canada ◦ HABITAT Forests ◦
FOOD Voles, other small mammals, birds, reptiles, frogs, eggs ◦ ACTIVE 🌃 🌅

Fast and graceful, the American Marten can chase its prey through the trees or on the ground. It is a slender animal with long, shiny dark brown fur. Its head is gray, with a pointed nose and small ears, and its legs are dark. Its tail is long and bushy. American Martens eat voles and squirrels, but they will also chow down on a wide range of food from birds to insects and from fruit to nuts. For most of the year, they live by themselves in the forest. In spring, the females have one litter of one to five youngsters. American Martens once lived through much of the United States, but as forests have been cut down, their numbers have dropped.

NAME GAME

Many people know this animal by the common name of Pine Marten, but that name really only applies to the European Pine Marten (*Martes martes*). It lives in northern climates where it finds shelter in pines and other coniferous trees.

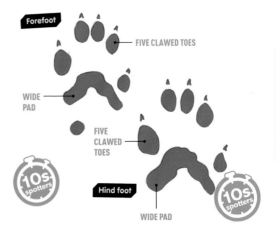

Forefoot

FIVE CLAWED TOES

WIDE PAD

FIVE CLAWED TOES

Hind foot

WIDE PAD

10s spotters

10s spotters

Fisher

Pekania pennanti LENGTH 2.6–3.3 ft (0.8–1 m) • RANGE Canada, Alaska, northeastern U.S., western mountains • HABITAT Forests • FOOD Porcupines, rodents, other small mammals, birds • ACTIVE **B** **L**

FOREFOOT: LARGE, WITH FIVE CLAWED TOES

HIND FOOT: LARGE, WITH FIVE CLAWED TOES

Few animals dare to attack a prickly North American Porcupine—but the Fisher does! This weasel strikes at the porcupine's face to kill and eat it. Fishers are long, slender, thickly furred animals with dark brown bodies; grizzled, grayish faces; and long, bushy tails. Once heavily hunted by trappers, their numbers are now growing slowly, and sometimes people spot them in yards and parks. In forests, they move quickly and easily on the ground or through the trees, often sleeping in tree hollows or in burrows. In spring, females bear one to six young in a protected den.

NAME GAME

Fishers rarely eat fish! Their name may come from a lookalike European weasel called a Fitchet.

FOREFOOT: WIDE, WITH FOUR TOES PRINTING

Ermine

Mustela erminea LENGTH 7–12 in (17.8–30.5 cm) • RANGE Canada, Alaska, western mountain states, upper Midwest, Northeast • HABITAT Forests • FOOD Rabbits, rodents, other small mammals, frogs • ACTIVE **N** **L**

HIND FOOT: LONG, WITH FOUR TOES PRINTING

This handsome little weasel is so slim and quick that it can chase its prey down burrows and cracks. It is energetic and hungry, often killing more than it can eat at one time. It stores the extra food in an underground room near its den. Ermine, also known as Short-tailed Weasels or Stoats, are dark brown on top and white on their bellies. In northern areas, their shiny fur turns all white in winter, except for the black tip on their tails. Like most weasels, they have long bodies, short legs, and pointed faces. Every spring, they have one litter of four to nine youngsters.

HIND FOOT: LONG, WITH FOUR TOES PRINTING

Long-tailed Weasel

Mustela frenata **LENGTH 11–22 in (28–56 cm)** • **RANGE Canada, most of U.S. except desert Southwest** • **HABITAT Woods, fields, farms** • **FOOD Rodents, rabbits, other small animals, fruits, berries** • **ACTIVE 🅑 🅛**

The Long-tailed Weasel can be found across most of the United States, living in burrows around woods and fields. It is a fierce and fearless hunter. As it chases its prey, it bounds over and over again into the air with its back curved. Then it bites its victim in the back of the neck and curls its long body around it. Long-tailed Weasels are slender, with short legs and long, bushy, black-tipped tails. Their colors vary from brown to orange, with white bellies. Northern Long-tailed Weasels turn white in winter. Females have one litter of four to eight young in the spring.

FOREFOOT: WIDE, WITH FOUR TOES PRINTING

Laugh Out Loud!

A weasel sits down in a restaurant and asks for something to drink. "What would you like?" asks the waitress. "Water, milk, or pop?"

"Pop," goes the weasel.

HIND FOOT: SMALL AND NARROW, WITH FOUR TOES PRINTING

Least Weasel

Mustela nivalis **LENGTH 7–8 in (17.8–20.3 cm)** • **RANGE Canada, north-central U.S., mid-Atlantic states** • **HABITAT Fields, marshes, forests** • **FOOD Mice, voles, other small animals, eggs** • **ACTIVE 🅑 🅛**

The tiny Least Weasel is the smallest carnivore in the world. The skinny mammal is no longer than a pencil, but it hunts down and eats animals its own size or even larger. It has to eat at least half its body weight in food every day to survive. Aside from their size, these little predators are typical weasels. They have long, slender bodies and short legs, with triangular-shaped heads, small ears, and short tails. Their fur is brown on top and white below. In the North, their coats turn completely white in winter. Least Weasels live in burrows left behind by other mammals, where females have up to three litters a year of one to six babies.

FOREFOOT: SMALL BUT WIDE, WITH FOUR TOES PRINTING

Black-footed Ferret

Mustela nigripes LENGTH 20–23 in (51–58.5 cm) • RANGE
South Dakota, Arizona, Wyoming • HABITAT Dry prairies • FOOD
Prairie dogs, small mammals • ACTIVE **N E**

Once fairly common across the
American plains, the Black-footed
Ferret became almost extinct in
the wild by the 1980s. With a few
survivors, scientists have bred
these members of the weasel family
in captivity and returned them to the
prairie in a few places, hoping they will
breed and spread. Black-footed Ferrets are the
only wild ferrets in the world. They are slender and yellow-brown, with
dark feet, a dark tip on their tail, and a dark mask across their eyes.
They breed once a year, with females having three to five young in a
litter. They are very dependent on prairie dogs (pages 26–27) both for
food and for homes: They take over prairie dog burrows as living
spaces. In the 20th century, Black-footed Ferrets faced a big problem.
As ranchers trapped and killed prairie dogs by the millions, Black-
footed Ferrets lost both food and shelter. Ferrets and prairie dogs
also began to die out from diseases, including sylvatic plague. Now
that some are back in the wild, these endangered mammals still face
challenges. About 300 live in a few protected spots in the West.

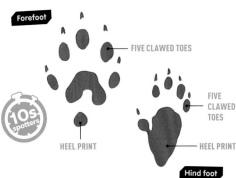

Forefoot

FIVE CLAWED TOES

HEEL PRINT

FIVE
CLAWED
TOES

HEEL PRINT

Hind foot

10s
spotters

Be an ANIMAL ACE!

Sometimes a hunting weasel will
hop backward and sideways and
roll about in front of its prey.
Sound nutty? This behavior may
confuse the prey!

American Mink

Vison vison **LENGTH 19–28 in (48.5–71 cm)** ▪ **RANGE Canada, most of U.S. except parts of Southwest** ▪ **HABITAT Wooded areas near water** ▪ **FOOD Small mammals, crayfish, fish, frogs** ▪ **ACTIVE** N L

The American Mink is a fierce and secretive predator. With its sleek, densely furred body and webbed toes, it is a fine swimmer and often preys on muskrats, fish, or even turtles. American Mink have long, slim bodies, with shiny dark brown fur marked by white patches on the chin, throat, and chest. They live in dens near water and often move from one den to the next. Like their cousins the weasels and skunks, American Mink can release a truly stinky spray, and they will mark the edges of their territories this way. Each spring, females give birth to one litter of one to ten young in a soft, fur-lined den.

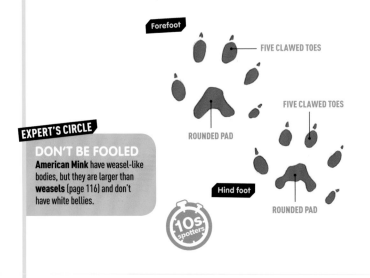

Forefoot

FIVE CLAWED TOES

FIVE CLAWED TOES

ROUNDED PAD

Hind foot

ROUNDED PAD

10s spotters

EXPERT'S CIRCLE

DON'T BE FOOLED

American Mink have weasel-like bodies, but they are larger than **weasels** (page 116) and don't have white bellies.

American Badger

Taxidea taxus LENGTH **20–34 in (51–86.5 cm)**
• RANGE **Western and central U.S., Canada** • HABITAT
Grasslands, meadows, farms, edges of woods • FOOD **Small
mammals, birds, snakes, frogs** • ACTIVE 🌓 🌙

The American Badger is made for a digging life. The forepaws on its short, strong legs are tipped with big claws. With them, the badger can dig a tunnel in minutes, uncovering prey or escaping from enemies. Badgers have wide, flat bodies with grizzled gray or brown fur and short, bushy tails. Their pointed faces have noticeable white stripes, one on each cheek and one running from the nose over the head to the back. They often hunt burrowing animals such as ground squirrels or even rattlesnakes. Sometimes a Coyote will wait nearby to snatch up a badger's escaping prey. Badgers spend a lot of time digging new dens and may move from one to the next every few days. In winter, they don't hibernate, but they do spend more time sleeping underground. Females give birth to a litter of one to five youngsters every spring.

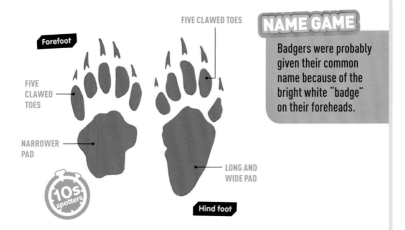

Forefoot

FIVE CLAWED TOES

FIVE CLAWED TOES

NARROWER PAD

LONG AND WIDE PAD

Hind foot

10s. spotters

NAME GAME

Badgers were probably given their common name because of the bright white "badge" on their foreheads.

American Hog-nosed Skunk

Conepatus leuconotus **LENGTH 20–36 in (51–91.5 cm)** • **RANGE Southwestern U.S.** • **HABITAT Deserts, canyons, brushy areas** • **FOOD Insects, worms, rodents, vegetables** • **ACTIVE** N L

FOREFOOT:
WIDE, FIVE CLAWED TOES

The American Hog-nosed Skunk does in fact have a hoglike nose. The nose is hairless and broad and good for rooting around in the ground, where the skunk digs up insects to eat. Texans call it the Rooter Skunk. This large skunk has a black face and a wide white stripe from its forehead to the tip of its tail. Its front legs are strong, with big claws. Like all skunks, it can spray attackers with a nasty smelling liquid from glands on its rump. Before it does that, though, it will try to run away or will face its enemy, hissing and stomping before it turns and sprays. Females give birth in dens among the rocks, producing one litter of two to four young each spring.

Hooded Skunk

HIND FOOT:
LONG, WIDER AT THE FRONT;
FIVE CLAWED TOES

Mephitis macroura **LENGTH 22–31 in (56–79 cm)** • **RANGE Southern Arizona and New Mexico, West Texas** • **HABITAT Canyons, deserts, brushy stream banks** • **FOOD Insects, rodents, birds** • **ACTIVE** N L

The Hooded Skunk lives in the hot, dry lands of the far Southwest. It's "hooded" because long hairs on the back of its neck form a kind of hood behind its face. Hooded skunks have one or two broad white stripes running down their back and sides and a sharp narrow white stripe running from forehead to nose. Their big bushy tails can be a mix of black and white hairs. They spend the day in their dens and then scout about at night

FOREFOOT:
ROUNDED, FIVE CLAWED TOES

looking for insects or other small animals to eat. When threatened, they make a classic skunk move: They run a short distance, raise their tails, and spray. Females have one litter of three to five young in late spring.

Striped Skunk

Mephitis mephitis LENGTH **20–31 in (51–79 cm)** · RANGE **Canada, all of U.S. except driest deserts** · HABITAT **Woods, fields, suburbs** · FOOD **Insects, small mammals, other small animals, eggs, plants** · ACTIVE **N** **L**

The Striped Skunk is one of the best known mammals in the country. It is famous not only for its bold black-and-white coat but also for its super-stinky spray. Striped Skunks have black fur, with a broad white stripe running from the top of their heads to their tails, often splitting into two stripes in the middle. Their foreheads are marked with a thin white stripe as well. They are adaptable animals that fit into a wide range of habitats. Trotting about at night, they will eat almost anything, from insects to plants to dead animals. When they're threatened, they hiss and stomp their forefeet. If the other animal doesn't back off, they turn around and let loose with an extremely smelly spray. Not only is this oily spray hard to wash off, but if it gets in the eyes it stings and blinds the victim for a short time. Striped Skunks live in dens in protected places, sometimes under houses, where the females have one litter of four to seven young in spring.

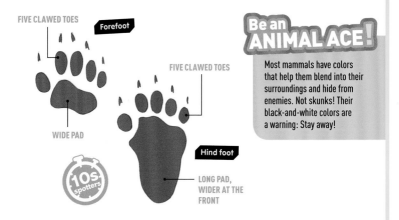

FIVE CLAWED TOES

Forefoot

FIVE CLAWED TOES

WIDE PAD

10s. spotters

Hind foot

LONG PAD, WIDER AT THE FRONT

Be an ANIMAL ACE!

Most mammals have colors that help them blend into their surroundings and hide from enemies. Not skunks! Their black-and-white colors are a warning: Stay away!

Western Spotted Skunk

Spilogale gracilis LENGTH 12–17 in (30.5–43 cm) • RANGE Canada, western U.S. • HABITAT Rocky areas, woodlands, farmlands • FOOD Small mammals, insects, snakes, eggs • ACTIVE 🌙 🌓

Small and trim, the Western Spotted Skunk is a handsome animal. Its black, silky coat is marked with broken white stripes and spots from head to rump. A bright white spot dots its forehead and the fluffy tail has a white tip. These skunks live in dens in old burrows, logs, rocks, or even in attics. They are good climbers and diggers and eager hunters, eating mice, insects, and other small creatures. When they're threatened, they warn their enemies by stomping their feet. If the enemy doesn't retreat, they do a handstand on their front legs and wave their tails to say "watch out!" If the enemy keeps coming, they drop their hind legs to the ground and zap the intruder with their smelly spray. Western Spotted Skunks have litters of two to five kits each spring.

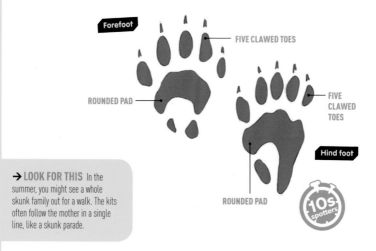

Forefoot

FIVE CLAWED TOES

ROUNDED PAD

FIVE CLAWED TOES

Hind foot

ROUNDED PAD

10s spotters

→ **LOOK FOR THIS** In the summer, you might see a whole skunk family out for a walk. The kits often follow the mother in a single line, like a skunk parade.

Ringtail

Bassariscus astutus LENGTH 26–31 in (66–79 cm) • RANGE Southwestern U.S. • HABITAT Canyons and other rocky areas, woods • FOOD Small mammals, insects, reptiles, plants • ACTIVE ◐ ◐

The graceful Ringtail is an excellent climber, even on rocks. Its hind feet can turn halfway around, and that together with sharp claws and rough foot pads allows it to run quickly up and down trees and cliffs. Ringtails have slender bodies, with yellow-brown fur on top and paler fur on their bellies. Their pointed faces have big dark eyes inside pale rings. True to their name, their tails are long and ringed from top to bottom in black and white bands. At night, Ringtails prowl the canyons and woods of the Southwest, hunting a wide variety of animals, but they also snack on fruit and other plants. In late spring, they give birth to one litter of one to five young.

NAME GAME

Gold miners used to keep Ringtails in their camps to catch mice. That is why they are sometimes known as Miner's Cats.

Forefoot

FIVE CLAWED TOES

WIDE PAD WITH HEEL PRINT

FIVE CLAWED TOES

Hind foot

10s spotters

WIDE PAD

Raccoon

Procyon lotor **LENGTH 24–37 in (61–94 cm)** ▪ **RANGE Canada, most of U.S. except for parts of West** ▪ **HABITAT Woods, wetlands, suburbs, cities** ▪ **FOOD Small mammals, insects, reptiles, fish, plants** ▪ **ACTIVE ◑ ◐**

The clever Raccoon is an adaptable animal, found in a wide variety of habitats across most of the United States. With its grizzled grayish fur, black mask across the eyes, and banded bushy tail, it is a familiar sight in many yards and woods. Raccoons' long fingers can not only handle food but also open doors, pull lids off garbage cans, and untie knots. It is a myth that Raccoons wash their food, although they sometimes hold their food under water while they pick at it. Raccoons are excellent climbers that make their dens in trees, boulders, or even houses. They scout around for food mostly at night, eating almost anything from fruit to frogs to eggs to animals killed on the road. When cornered by other animals, they are fierce fighters whose screams can be heard far away. In winter, Raccoons don't hibernate, but they do sleep in their dens. Females give birth to one or more litters of two to seven cubs per year in spring.

TRY THIS!

Can you name an animal from this book by its tracks? Try it!

1. Hint: A toothy tree cruncher

2. Hint: A stripe-faced digger

3. Hint: An armored animal

4. Hint: A sleeper in winter

5. Hint: A heavyweight of the West

1. American Beaver (page 41)
2. American Badger (page 119)
3. Nine-banded Armadillo (page 17)
4. American Black Bear (page 110)
5. American Bison (page 141)

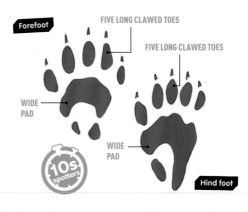

Forefoot

FIVE LONG CLAWED TOES

FIVE LONG CLAWED TOES

WIDE PAD

WIDE PAD

Hind foot

10s spotters

Harbor Seal

Phoca vitulina LENGTH 4–6.2 ft (1.2–1.9 m) • RANGE
East Coast from Canada to the Carolinas, West Coast
from Alaska through California • HABITAT Coastal
waters, beaches, lakes • FOOD Fish, squid, crabs,
shrimp • ACTIVE 🌙 🌓

Go for a stroll along rocky
beaches in New England or
California, and you may surprise
a resting Harbor Seal. The ocean
mammal will probably bark and
slither into the water; although some
are used to visitors, most Harbor Seals are
shy. Harbor Seals are smooth and sturdy, rounded out by a thick layer
of fat under their skin. They have four long, flat flippers that move
them easily through the water and awkwardly on land. Their coats can
be light with dark spots or black with light rings. They have big shiny
eyes and no visible ears. Stiff whiskers spread out from their noses.
Although they need to breathe air, Harbor Seals can dive deep and
stay under the water for almost half an hour. When they're done with
the water, they will rest on a beach—an action called hauling out—
sometimes in family groups. Females give birth to one or two pups
once a year.

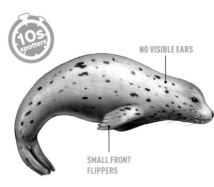

NO VISIBLE EARS

SMALL FRONT
FLIPPERS

Be an ANIMAL ACE!

They're fast in the water, but
Harbor Seals still have some
deadly enemies. Sharks,
Killer Whales, and in the North,
Polar Bears, will prey on them.
Sometimes Coyotes attack
pups on the beach.

MAMMAL MANIA: UNDER THE SEA

PACIFIC WHITE-SIDED DOLPHINS SWIM IN WATERS OFF THE COAST OF BRITISH COLUMBIA.

Hundreds of millions of years ago, animals left the sea to live on land. Around 50 million years ago, some mammals went back. Different kinds of doglike, elephant-like, and hippo-like creatures reentered the water and eventually evolved into the seals, manatees, and whales, respectively, we know today. These ocean creatures are still mammals: They are warm-blooded and feed their young with milk. They have to breathe air. They are wonderfully adapted, though, to life in a watery world.

Sleek and Streamlined

Sea mammal bodies have smooth shapes that slide easily through water. Their ears don't stick out and they have short fur or just a sprinkling of hair. Their limbs have evolved from legs into flat fins and flippers. A thick layer of fat under the skin keeps them warm in cold waters. Most marine mammals have pale bellies that blend into the bright surface when seen from below, and dark backs that blend into the sea when seen from above. This helps protect them from predators such as sharks.

Deep Divers

All sea mammals have to come to the surface to breathe—but they don't have to do it as often as a human would. Dolphins need to breathe every few minutes, but some whales and seals can stay underwater for more than an hour. When seals dive deep, their lungs collapse and breathing stops. Their bodies can store more oxygen than the bodies of land animals, and while diving their oxygen-carrying blood goes mainly to the organs that need it most, such as the brain and heart. Their heart rates can drop to only four or five beats per minute, like those of an animal in deep hibernation.

Singing in the Deep

It's hard to see far underwater, but sound carries well. Ocean mammals rely on sound to send messages and to find their way around. Whales whistle, creak, and moan in complex patterns. Some of their very low pitched calls, below the range of human hearing, can travel for thousands of miles in the water. Like bats, whales and dolphins use clicking sounds for echolocation. The sounds bounce off objects and return to their ears. The time it takes for the echo to return tells them how far away the object is and even its shape.

California Sea Lion

Zalophus californianus LENGTH 4.9–8.2 ft (1.5–2.5 m) ◦ RANGE West Coast from Vancouver through California ◦ HABITAT Coastal waters, beaches, islands ◦ FOOD Fish, squid ◦ ACTIVE 🌞 🌙

The clever, playful California Sea Lion lives along the coast of California, although many people know it from zoos, where it jumps and tosses balls with zookeepers. Long and slender, it has short brown fur on top with a lighter belly; a female is paler than a male. A California Sea Lion's slender snout is whiskery and it has small, visible ears. Four black flippers help it swim swiftly and gracefully. On land, California Sea Lions walk on their flippers and can gallop around fairly easily. Swimming after fish, they can dive as deep as 450 feet (137 m). In summer, they live in large breeding colonies, where the males fight each other to defend their own areas. Females give birth to one pup the following June. In winter, males migrate north and return to the breeding beaches in late spring.

EXPERT'S CIRCLE

DON'T BE FOOLED Not sure if you're looking at a California **Sea Lion** or a **Harbor Seal** (page 125)? Check the ears and flippers. California Sea Lions have visible ears straight back from their eyes and long front flippers. Harbor Seals have no visible ears and smaller front flippers.

SMALL VISIBLE EARS

LONG FRONT FLIPPERS

NARROW SNOUT

10s. spotters

Humpback Whale

Megaptera novaeangliae **LENGTH 48–62.5 ft (14.5–19 m)**
• **RANGE West and northeast coasts, Canada and U.S.** • **HABITAT Polar to tropical ocean waters** • **FOOD Fish, shrimp, plankton**
• **ACTIVE** Ⓓ Ⓛ Ⓔ

The majestic Humpback Whale lives in oceans around the world. People in the United States see them off the west and northeastern coasts in the spring through fall. These beautiful mammals are baleen whales, which means they don't have teeth. Instead they have comblike plates in their jaws that they use to filter food from the water. They are dark, with patches of white. Their heads are covered with little knobs, and their flippers are very long and slender. Although Humpbacks can stay underwater for at least 30 minutes, usually they surface every 7 to 15 minutes to breathe through two blowholes on their heads. Sometimes they leap right out of the water, a habit called breaching. Humpbacks swim about 16,000 miles (25,750 km) each year, feeding in northern waters and giving birth in southern oceans. Females have one calf each winter. In past centuries, whalers killed so many that Humpbacks became endangered. Now they are protected and their numbers are growing, though they still face many challenges. Most populations have been taken off the endangered species list.

FROM BLOWHOLE SPOUTS ROUNDED CLOUD

LONG BLACK-AND-WHITE FLIPPERS

Be an
ANIMAL ACE!

Humpback Whales are famous for their haunting songs, which can be heard for miles underwater. Only the male Humpbacks sing, but all the Humpbacks in one group sing the same song that gradually changes over time. No one really knows why they sing.

Gray Whale

Eschrichtius robustus **LENGTH 45–49 ft (13.5–15 m)** • **RANGE West Coast from Alaska to California** • **HABITAT Polar to warm oceans, often in shallow water** • **FOOD Small ocean animals, tube worms** • **ACTIVE** ● ● ●

The Gray Whale is one of the few whales you might commonly see close to shore. These whales like to feed on little creatures in shallow waters, such as krill. Turning on their sides, the whales scrape along the ocean floor and scoop vast amounts of sand and food into their huge mouths. Gray Whales, like Humpbacks, are baleen whales, with plates instead of teeth. They are slender, with gray patchy skin and long, narrow heads. Like Humpbacks, they breathe through two blowholes on the back of their heads. These long-distance swimmers migrate thousands of miles between their feeding grounds near Alaska and their breeding areas off the coast of Mexico. In these warm waters, females give birth to one calf in January. They guard their calves fiercely and will even attack ships that come too close to them. Gray Whales are protected from most hunting, but one population in Asia is endangered.

FROM BLOWHOLE SPOUTS SHORT, HEART-SHAPED CLOUD

KNUCKLE-LIKE KNOBS ON ITS BACK

10s spotters

→ **LOOK FOR THIS** If you're lucky enough to spot a **GRAY WHALE,** you may see it do a typical whale move called spy-hopping. The whale will poke its head straight up out of the water, using its flippers to keep it above the surface. It may either be looking around or listening—curious about prey or enemies or even human visitors.

Killer Whale

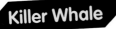

TALL BLACK FIN ON MALES

Orcinus orca **LENGTH 23–32 ft (7–10 m)** • **RANGE East and West Coasts, Canada and U.S.** • **HABITAT Cool, near-shore water** • **FOOD Seals, sea lions, other ocean mammals, fish, squids, turtles** • **ACTIVE** 🌞 **E**

GRAY SADDLE PATCHES ON BACK

Killer Whales, also known as Orcas, are true to their name. They are strong, fierce, smart predators that chase and eat everything from seals to birds. Killer Whales bite their prey, ram it, slap it with their tails, or leap out of the water and land on it to crush it. They even chase prey up onto a beach and then wiggle their way back to the water again. These are the largest dolphins, with sleek bodies, black backs, and large white spots. Males have a straight triangular back fin, while females have a smaller curved back fin. Killer whales live in family pods with up to 50 members and are led by a mother or grandmother. The pod works as a group to hunt its prey. Although Killer Whales live around the world, the pods in the U.S. Northwest are considered endangered due to threats to their habitat and loss of prey.

....

TALL CURVED FIN

Common Bottlenose Dolphin

Tursiops truncatus **LENGTH 8.5–11 ft (2.6–3.5 m)** • **RANGE East Coast from New Jersey south; Southern California coast** • **HABITAT Warmer ocean waters, bays, river mouths** • **FOOD Fish, eels, squid** • **ACTIVE** 🌙 **L**

Smart, speedy, and graceful, Common Bottlenose Dolphins are a favorite sight as they curve through the water just off shore. These ocean mammals are dark to light gray with paler bellies and long flippers. A tall, curved fin rises from their backs; their heads are rounded, with long bottle-shaped beaks. Their muscular, streamlined bodies make them swift, and they can swim up to 18 miles an hour (29 km/h) at times. With big brains, these dolphins are highly intelligent. They learn quickly and communicate with each other using whistling sounds. Common Bottlenose Dolphins are also very social, living in groups of up to 100. Females give birth to one calf every three to six years.

BOTTLE-SHAPED BEAK

Short-beaked Common Dolphin

Delphinus delphis LENGTH 6.2–8.2 ft (1.9–2.5 m) • RANGE Canada and U.S., East and West Coasts • HABITAT Mild to warm ocean waters • FOOD Fish, squid • ACTIVE **B** **L**

HOURGLASS-SHAPED PATCH ON SIDES

LONG BEAK

Surfing in front of boats, leaping out of the water, somersaulting, the Short-beaked Common Dolphin loves to play in the water. This lively ocean mammal is found in much of the world, including near the Atlantic and Pacific coasts of the United States. It is more colorful than most dolphins, with a dark back, pale underside, and a tan and gray hourglass-shaped patch on its sides. Its beak is long and pointed. These social animals travel in large schools made up of hundreds or even thousands of members. They take care of each other and will hold up a sick dolphin on their fins so it can breathe. Old stories tell of these dolphins even helping injured human swimmers the same way. Female dolphins have one calf every one to three years. The baby stays close to its mother for more than a year.

West Indian Manatee

LONG FLEXIBLE FRONT FLIPPERS

THICK SQUARE SNOUT

Trichechus manatus LENGTH 8–13 ft (2.4–4 m) • RANGE Florida coast, East Coast to Virginia, Gulf Coast to Louisiana • HABITAT Warm ocean waters, shallow rivers, bays • FOOD Seagrasses, algae • ACTIVE **B** **T**

The mild-mannered, slow-moving West Indian Manatee favors the warm salt or fresh waters around the Florida coast. Also called Sea Cow for its thick body and love of plants, it has wrinkled gray skin and a split upper lip. Its two front flippers look almost like arms, and its broad tail can push it through the water at up to 15 miles an hour (24 km/h). It is rarely in a hurry, though. Manatees spend six to eight hours a day grazing on plants in shallow water. Females have one or two calves every three to five years. Although these big mammals have no natural enemies, water pollution and accidents with boat propellers killed so many that they were once endangered. They are on the way to recovery but are still listed as threatened.

Wild Boar

Sus scrofa **LENGTH 4.3–6 ft (1.3–1.8 m) ▪ RANGE New Hampshire, scattered groups in South and West ▪ HABITAT Forests, brushlands, swamps, mountains ▪ FOOD Roots, nuts, fruit, eggs, small animals ▪ ACTIVE 🅑 🅛**

Wild Boars are not native to North America. They were brought here in the 19th and 20th centuries by people who wanted to hunt them in the American wild. Soon they escaped and began to breed with farm pigs. Now these feral animals live by the millions in New England and in the South and West. Wild Boars are husky animals with coarse brown or black hair, which sometimes sticks up in a ruff down their backs. Their faces end in a round, soft snout, which is flanked by two long, upward-curving teeth. Straight, narrow legs end in sharp hooves. These pigs do a lot of damage to the land. They pull up and trample plants, including farm crops, and they wallow in the mud. Females and piglets travel in groups called sounders, but males are usually alone. Females have one to two litters a year of five to six piglets each.

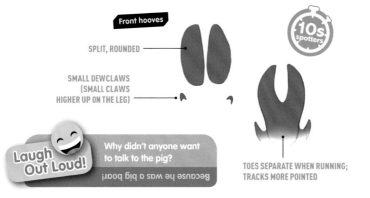

Front hooves

SPLIT, ROUNDED

SMALL DEWCLAWS (SMALL CLAWS HIGHER UP ON THE LEG)

10 s. Spotters

TOES SEPARATE WHEN RUNNING; TRACKS MORE POINTED

Laugh Out Loud!
Why didn't anyone want to talk to the pig?
Because he was a big boar!

Collared Peccary

Pecari tajacu LENGTH 3–3.3 ft (0.9–1 m) • RANGE Southern Arizona, southwestern New Mexico, southern Texas • HABITAT Deserts, canyons, brushy areas • FOOD Cacti, shrubs, roots, nuts • ACTIVE 🄱 🄻

HIND HOOF: SMALLER, ROUNDED SPLIT OVALS

FRONT HOOF: ROUNDED, SPLIT OVALS

These social, piglike animals live in dry regions of the Southwest. They are covered with short, grizzled gray or black hair, with a pale yellow band circling their necks like a collar. Big heads and shoulders taper down to small hind ends, and their slender legs end in hooves. Peccaries have piglike snouts and short tusks that look like little spears or javelins, which gives them their other common name: Javelina. They live in groups of 5 to 15 animals that spend all their time together, eating cacti and other plants and sleeping as a herd. One male will be in charge of the group, and both males and females will defend their territory from other Collared Peccaries. Females have one litter a year of two to six young.

Moose

Alces americanus LENGTH 6.8–9.2 ft (2–2.8 m) • RANGE Canada, Alaska, Rocky Mountains, north-central U.S., New England • HABITAT Northern forests, tundra, swamps • FOOD Leaves, twigs, bark, water plants • ACTIVE 🄱 🄻

FRONT AND BACK HOOVES: LONG, POINTED, SPLIT PRINTS

The ruler of the northern forest, the Moose is the world's biggest member of the deer family. A male Moose (a bull) can stand 7.5 feet (2.3 m) tall at its shoulder and weigh 1,400 pounds (635 kg). They are striking, with dark brown hair, long lanky legs, and humped shoulders. Their heads are very long, with a curved nose and a flap of skin, called a dewlap, hanging from their necks. The males' broad, flat antlers can span more than six feet (1.8 m) from side to side. Moose shed antlers every winter and grow new ones each spring. In summer, they spend time in water, staying cool and eating plants. In winter, they munch on trees. Females (called cows) have one to two calves each year and protect them fiercely.

DANGER!

If Moose feel threatened they can charge! Stay away. If one charges you, run behind a tree to protect yourself.

Mule Deer

Odocoileus hemionus **LENGTH 4–7.5 ft (1.2–2.3 m)**
RANGE Canada, southwestern Alaska, western U.S **HABITAT
Deserts, forests, mountains** **FOOD Twigs, bark, leaves, nuts,
berries** **ACTIVE** ⬤ ⬤

Its long, twitchy ears, like those
of a mule, give the Mule Deer
its name. This western deer is
stocky, with long legs and a coat
that can range from gray to
reddish. Pale patches mark its
throat, rump, and the insides of its
legs. Males have branched antlers,
which fall off and then grow back
larger every year. Mule Deer are out in the
day and night, grazing on plants and watching
for predators such as Mountain Lions or wolves. They have good
hearing and vision, and when they spot an enemy they bound
away quickly. During breeding season, males will fight, locking
their antlers together and pushing back and forth. If their
antlers can't be untangled, sometimes they starve to death.
Females give birth to one or two fawns in the summer. The fawns'
spotted coats help them stay hidden in the brush until they are
a few months old and can travel around with their mothers.

Front and back hooves

10s
spotters

LONG,
POINTED,
SPLIT
PRINTS

→ **LOOK FOR THIS** When
a **MULE DEER** spots danger,
it may run away in a series of
bounds called stotting. It leaps
into the air with all four feet off
the ground and its legs remain
straight and stiff below it. This
bouncy run may send a message
to predators that the Mule Deer
will be hard to catch.

White-tailed Deer

Odocoileus virginianus LENGTH 5.3–7.2 ft (1.6–2.2 m) • RANGE Canada, U.S. except far Southwest • HABITAT Woods, farms, brushy areas, suburbs • FOOD Twigs, leaves, shrubs, nuts, fruit • ACTIVE 🅑 🅛

White-tailed Deer are now widespread and common, but once they were extinct in much of the United States. Overhunting by early settlers wiped out many of these deer, but with better hunting rules the animals have come back in a big way. About 15 million live across the country today. White-taileds are small to medium-size deer. Their short fur is grayish in winter and reddish in summer, with white on their throats and bellies. Males, called bucks, grow antlers every spring and shed them each winter. In their first year, they grow only small spikes. Their short tails are white on the underside, and the deer will flip them up and jump away at the first sign of danger. White-tailed Deer are fast and graceful, able to spring over fences 8.5 feet (2.6 m) high and cover 30 feet (9 m) in one bound. Females, called does, give birth to one to three fawns in the spring.

Be an ANIMAL ACE!

A subspecies of White-tailed Deer known as the Key Deer lives only on the islands of the Florida Keys. At one point only 25 of this tiny deer, no bigger than a dog, remained alive. Now it is listed as endangered, and under protection their numbers are growing. About 700 to 800 live on the islands, although they still face danger from human visitors and their cars.

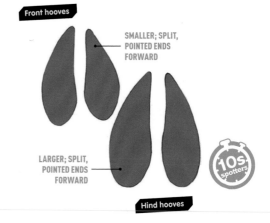

Front hooves

SMALLER; SPLIT, POINTED ENDS FORWARD

LARGER; SPLIT, POINTED ENDS FORWARD

Hind hooves

10s. spotters

Caribou

Rangifer tarandus LENGTH 4.5–8.2 ft (1.4–2.5 m) · RANGE Canada, Alaska, Washington, Idaho · HABITAT Northern forest, tundra · FOOD Grasses, shrubs, lichens · ACTIVE 🅐 🅛 🅔

FRONT AND BACK HOOVES: WIDELY SPACED CRESCENTS; DEWCLAW MARKS

Caribou, big deer of the far north, are major migrators like their Reindeer relatives of northern Europe. In spring, huge herds of thousands of caribou travel hundreds of miles north to calving grounds, where they give birth to their young. In the fall, herds migrate south with the young to their more sheltered winter range. Caribou have brown fur on their heads, bodies, and legs, while their necks, bellies, and rumps are pale. Their large hooves have sharp edges, good for digging for food in the snow. They are the only members of the deer family in which both males and females have antlers, although the males' antlers are bigger and broader than the females'. Females have one or two calves a year. These youngsters are able to run within 90 minutes of their birth. Caribou are widespread in Alaska, but endangered in Idaho and Washington State.

Elk

Cervus elaphus LENGTH 6.6–9.8 ft (2–3 m) · RANGE Canada, Rocky Mountains into Southwest; Washington, Montana, Wyoming, Colorado; scattered groups in upper Midwest and East · HABITAT Open meadows, woods, mountain slopes · FOOD Grasses, woody plants · ACTIVE 🅑 🅛

FRONT AND BACK HOOVES: LARGE AND SPLIT, POINTED ENDS FORWARD

These big, handsome members of the deer family are also known as Wapiti. Once they roamed most of the United States and Canada. Overhunting and loss of habitat drove down their numbers into the 20th century and they vanished from many places. Now, with better care, Elk herds are growing again and they especially thrive in parts of the East, such as northeastern Pennsylvania's Elk County. Elk are tall, sturdy, light-brown mammals with a dark brown mane on their throats and a pale patch on their rumps. Males (bulls) have large antlers. Females (cows) and their calves gather in big herds. In the fall, bulls take over the herds and defend them against other males: The males smack their heads and antlers together, but the fighters are rarely hurt. In spring, females give birth to a single calf.

MAMMAL MANIA: RECORD HOLDERS

Fastest

As soon as it spots danger, the Pronghorn (page 140) moves like lightning. This long-legged animal of the American West can sprint at up to 60 miles an hour (96 km/h), which makes it the second fastest land animal in the world after the African Cheetah.

BUFFALO IN WYOMING'S HAYDEN VALLEY

North America has some of the biggest, smallest, and speediest mammals on Earth. Take a look at the record holders on this page, starting with the American Bison (page 141). You would not want this animal to step on your toes! Also called Buffalo, it is the biggest land mammal in the country. Adult males can stand six feet (1.8 m) tall at their humped shoulders and weigh up to one ton (907 kg). Calves weigh between 30 and 70 pounds (14–32 kg) at birth. Hunted to near extinction in the late 1800s, bison have made a comeback across the United States.

Smallest and Shortest-Lived

The super-tiny American Pygmy Shrew is no larger than a big bumblebee. It may grow to no more than two inches (5 cm) long and weigh about as much as a dime. This little-known creature may also be the shortest-lived mammal in North America, living about one year.

Longest-Lived

Some American land mammals, such as the Grizzly Bear (page 111), can live up to 30 years. But to find the truly long-lived mammals, you have to dive into the ocean. Swimming through Alaska waters and other cold seas, Bowhead Whales can live more than 200 years.

Biggest in Prehistory

The earliest humans in North America shared the land with one of the biggest mammals ever: the Columbian Mammoth. This ancient relative of the elephant was 13 feet (4 m) tall at the shoulders and weighed 11 tons (10 t). Its pointed, curving tusks could be 16 feet (5 m) long. The enormous animal became extinct around 11,500 years ago.

Pronghorn

Antilocapra americana LENGTH 4.3–5 ft (1.3–1.5 m) • RANGE Canada, western U.S. • HABITAT Open grasslands, deserts • FOOD Grasses, cacti, shrubs • ACTIVE 🌑 🌓

The Pronghorn is the fastest mammal in North America. It can run at 60 miles an hour (96 km/h) for short distances, and at a steady 30 miles an hour (48 km/h) for long distances. This unique animal is the only surviving member of a family that goes back 50 million years to prehistoric North America. It isn't a deer, but it looks like one, with a barrel-shaped body, long legs, and a slender, pointed head. Pronghorn are tan, with white bands on their cheeks, throats, sides, and bellies. Both males and females have black horns with short prongs sticking forward about halfway up, although female horns are short or sometimes not visible. On their rumps they have long white hairs that they flash when they run. Their big, round eyes have excellent vision. Pronghorn live out in the open in large herds in winter and smaller herds in summer. Females have one or two young in early summer. Within days, the youngsters can run faster than a human.

Be an ANIMAL ACE!

There's a difference between horns and antlers. Horns, such as those on Pronghorn, are made of bone on the inside and keratin (like fingernails) on the outside. Pronghorn shed the outer covering every year, but other horned animals, such as bison, keep the whole thing. Antlers, which are found on all members of the deer family, are a special kind of bone that grows out of the skull. Antlers are shed every year.

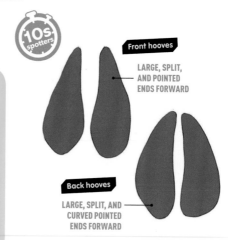

10s. spotters

Front hooves
LARGE, SPLIT, AND POINTED ENDS FORWARD

Back hooves
LARGE, SPLIT, AND CURVED POINTED ENDS FORWARD

American Bison

Bos bison LENGTH 6.6–12.5 ft (2–4 m) • RANGE Canada, Wyoming, Alaska, scattered parts of West • HABITAT Plains, prairies, woods • FOOD Grasses, brush • ACTIVE **B** **L**

Huge and heavy, the American Bison is the largest land mammal in North America. Once tens of millions of Bison lived across the country from the Atlantic to the Pacific. However, a binge of hunting in the 19th century drove them almost to extinction. Now, their numbers are growing, but they live almost entirely in protected places such as Yellowstone National Park or on private lands. American Bison look like no other animal. Their hair is dark brown and shaggy in front, but smoother in back. They have huge heads covered with curly thick hair, and high, humped shoulders. Sharp horns curve up from the tops of their heads on both males and females. Bison gather in herds that can have hundreds of members during mating season. If frightened, the herds stampede with a sound like thunder. Females have one calf each year, a youngster that is able to join the herd within days.

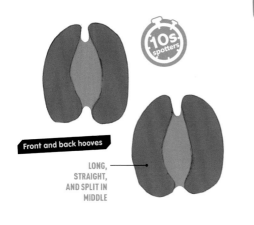

10s spotters

Front and back hooves

LONG, STRAIGHT, AND SPLIT IN MIDDLE

NAME GAME

Bison are often called Buffalo. The 17th-century explorer Samuel de Champlain gave them that name after seeing some bison hides. He seemed to think that the animals were closely related to African and Asian Buffalo, and the name caught on with American settlers.

Mountain Goat

Oreamnos americanus LENGTH 4.3–5.9 ft (1.3–1.8 m) • RANGE Canada, southern Alaska, Washington, Wyoming, Idaho, scattered spots in West • HABITAT Steep, rocky mountains • FOOD Mountain plants and shrubs • ACTIVE ☉ ☾

Leaping from ledge to ledge on high mountains, the Mountain Goat lives where most animals could not survive. Its hooves are adapted for climbing on cliffs—they can spread out on flat surfaces or close in around sharp rocks. Mountain Goats have thick, shaggy white fur and black eyes, noses, horns, and hooves. Their horns are short and as sharp as knives. They spend much of their lives on steep mountain-sides, where they are safe from most predators. Avalanches or rockslides are more likely to kill them. Females have one to three young in late spring. The babies can climb up mountain ledges within hours of their birth.

Front and back hooves

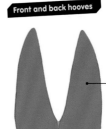

LONG, CURVED, SOMETIMES JOINED IN THE MIDDLE

TRY THIS!

Each mammal has its own special traits. Can you name these animals from this book?

1. I'm hungry and fierce and live in northern forests. With my strong jaws, I can chew through a metal trap. Who am I?

2. I'm small, but I'm danger-ous. My bite is venomous. Who am I?

3. Using my big front teeth, I can chop down trees and build a dam. Who am I?

4. My eyes are tiny and my nose is weird. With my wiggling tentacles, I look like an octopus. Who am I?

5. When I feel scared, I pretend to be dead. When the danger goes away, so do I. Who am I?

5. Virginia Opossum (page 16)
4. Star-nosed Mole (page 74)
3. American Beaver (page 41)
2. Northern Short-tailed Shrew (page 68)
1. Wolverine (page 113)

Bighorn Sheep

Ovis canadensis LENGTH 4.3–6.2 ft (1.3–1.9 m)
• RANGE Canada, Rocky Mountains into Southwest
• HABITAT Steep, rocky areas, deserts • FOOD Grasses,
woody plants • ACTIVE 🌞 🌓

Smash! Two Bighorn Sheep rear up and butt heads with a crash. Smash! They do it again. In mating season, male Bighorns smack heads over and over again at more than 20 miles an hour (32 hm/h). They can keep this up for hours for the right to mate with a female. Bighorn Sheep are natives of the cliffs and canyons of the rocky West. They are not as secure on rocks as Mountain Goats, but they can still balance on ledges only two inches (5 cm) wide. These muscular animals have tan to dark brown hair, with white bellies, rumps, and muzzles. Their hooves are soft in the middle, which helps them cling to rocks. Both females and males have horns, and the males' horns are enormous. Weighing up to 30 pounds (14 kg), they curl back from the forehead and around the sides of the cheeks. Bighorns travel in small groups, feeding on grasses and shrubs. Females have one lamb each spring.

Front and back hooves

LONG, STRAIGHT, SPLIT IN MIDDLE

Be an ANIMAL ACE!

If humans butted heads at the same speed as Bighorn Sheep, they would die. Bighorn Sheep horns and skulls are stronger and more flexible than human skulls. They bend and absorb the shock when heads clash. Bighorn brains also fill with extra blood during fights, which cushions the soft tissue.

Dall's Sheep

Ovis dalli LENGTH 3.3–4.9 ft (1–1.5 m) • RANGE Canada, Alaska • HABITAT High, rocky mountains • FOOD Grasses, woody plants • ACTIVE 🌣 🌙

These small but tough sheep live on the remote cliffs and slopes of Alaska mountains. They are white all over, with yellowish or brownish horns. In males, these horns can be huge and curve widely back from their foreheads. Female horns are thinner and straighter. Like their cousins the Bighorn Sheep, male Dall's Sheep fight head to head during mating season, rearing up and clashing with a loud smack. For most of the year, grown males travel in separate groups from females and their young. Females have one to two lambs each year. These young- sters can stand and follow their mothers on cliffs within hours.

FRONT AND BACK HOOVES: POINTED, SPLIT TRACKS

Wild Donkey

Equus asinus LENGTH 6.5 ft (2 m) • RANGE Southwest • HABITAT Deserts, canyons, moun- tains • FOOD Grasses, shrubs, cacti • ACTIVE 🌣 🌙

Wild Donkeys, also known as Burros, are not native to North America. As working animals, they were brought to this continent by early Spanish settlers in the 16th century, and then again by gold miners in the 19th century. Some escaped into the Southwest and formed feral, or wild, herds that live there to this day. Donkeys are close relatives of horses. They have shaggy fur that ranges in color from red to brown to gray, often with white snouts, and stiff manes. Their ears are long and their tails have a tuft at the ends. Their ancestors were desert animals, and Wild Donkeys do well in dry places, browsing on plants and getting by with little water. They are social and live in herds, where females raise one foal each year.

FRONT AND BACK HOOVES: LARGE, POINTED OVAL; TRIANGULAR NOTCH

NAME GAME

Donkeys can mate with horses, but their young are sterile—they can't have their own babies. When male donkeys mate with horses, their foal is called a mule. When female donkeys mate with horses, the foal is called a hinny.

Wild Horse

Equus caballus **HEIGHT AT SHOULDER 4.3–4.9 ft (1.3–1.5 m)**
**• RANGE West, southeastern barrier islands • HABITAT Brushlands,
mountains, islands • FOOD Grasses • ACTIVE** 🅑 🅛

Wild Horses roamed North
America in prehistoric times, but
by 10,000 to 8,000 years ago
they became extinct. Then, begin-
ning in the 16th century, Spanish
explorers and other early settlers
arrived with their own tame horses.
Some escaped into the wild in the West
and to barrier islands off the southeast
coast. Today, Wild Horses known as mustangs
roam the grasslands of the West. In the East, particularly on the islands
of Chincoteague and Assateague, herds of small horses live near the
beaches. Wild Horses tend to be smaller than farm horses, but otherwise
they look much the same. They have long heads, long manes and tails, and
big, semicircular hooves. Their shiny coats can range in color from white
to tan to brown to black. Wild Horses usually move in small herds led by a
male horse, or stallion. Females, or mares, can have one or two foals
about every other year.

Front and back hooves

LARGE OVAL;
SMALL
TRIANGULAR
NOTCH IN BACK

Be an ANIMAL ACE!

Wild horses pose a problem in
the West. On one hand, most
people like and admire the beautiful animals. On the other hand,
as their numbers grow, they
overgraze western grasslands.
As they eat the native grasses,
invasive grasses take their place,
which is bad for other plants and
animals. Wild Horses also compete for food and water with
other animals. People are now
trying to figure out how to control populations of Wild Horses
without hurting them.

OFFICIAL MAMMALS OF THE United States

WHITE-TAILED DEER Illinois

United States: American Bison

Alabama: American Black Bear

Alaska: Moose, Bowhead Whale

Arizona: Ringtail

Arkansas: White-tailed Deer

California: California Grizzly Bear, Gray Whale

Colorado: Rocky Mountain Bighorn Sheep

Connecticut: Sperm Whale

Delaware: Gray Fox

Florida: Florida Panther

Georgia: White-tailed Deer, Right Whale

Hawaii: Hawaiian Monk Seal

Idaho: Appaloosa Horse

Illinois: White-tailed Deer

Kansas: American Bison

Kentucky: Gray Squirrel

Louisiana: American Black Bear

Maine: Moose

Maryland: Calico Cat

Massachusetts: Right Whale

Michigan: White-tailed Deer

Mississippi: White-tailed Deer, Common Bottlenose Dolphin

AMERICAN BLACK BEAR Alabama

COYOTE South Dakota

Rhode Island: Harbor Seal

South Carolina: White-tailed Deer

South Dakota: Coyote

Tennessee: Raccoon

Texas: Nine-banded Armadillo, Mexican Free-tailed Bat

Utah: Rocky Mountain Elk

Vermont: Morgan Horse

Virginia: Virginia Big-eared Bat

Washington: Olympic Marmot, Killer Whale

West Virginia: American Black Bear

Wisconsin: Badger, White-tailed Deer

Wyoming: American Bison

Missouri: Missouri Mule

Montana: Grizzly Bear

Nebraska: White-tailed Deer

Nevada: Desert Bighorn Sheep

New Hampshire: White-tailed Deer

New Jersey: Horse

New Mexico: American Black Bear

New York: Beaver

North Carolina: Gray Squirrel

North Dakota: Nokota Horse

Ohio: White-tailed Deer

Oklahoma: American Bison, White-tailed Deer, Raccoon, Mexican Free-tailed Bat

Oregon: Beaver

Pennsylvania: White-tailed Deer

BEAVER New York

Quick ID Guide

OPOSSUMS AND ARMADILLOS

Virginia Opossum
Didelphidae 16

Nine-banded Armadillo
Dasypodidae 17

RODENTS

Mountain Beaver
Aplodontidae 18

Squirrels
Sciuridae 18

Beaver
Castoridae 41

New World Porcupines
Erethizontidae 44

**Kangaroo Rats and Pocket
Mice/Heteromyidae 44**

Pocket Gophers
Geomyidae 46

Jumping Mice
Dipodidae 46

New World Mice, Rats, and Voles/Cricetidae 48

Old World Mice and Rats Muridae 62

Nutria (Coypus) Echimyidae 67

Shrews Soricidae 68

Moles Talpidae 74

Pikas Ochotonidae 76

Hares and Rabbits Leporidae 77

New World Leaf-Nosed Bats Phyllostomidae 86

Free-tailed Bats Molossidae 87

Vesper Bats Vespertilionidae 89

CARNIVORES

Cats
Felidae 100

Dogs, Foxes, and Wolves
Canidae 104

Bears
Ursidae 110

Otters, Weasels, and Badgers
Mustelidae 112

Skunks
Mephitidae 120

Raccoons, Ringtails, and
Coatis/Procyonidae 123

Earless Seals
Phocidae 125

Eared Seals
Otariidae 128

WHALES, DOLPHINS & MANATEES

Rorquals
Balaenopteridae 129

Gray Whale
Eschrichtiidae 130

Dolphins
Delphinidae 131

Manatees
Trichechidae 132

HOOFED MAMMALS

Pigs
Suidae 133

Peccaries
Tayassuidae 134

Deer
Cervidae 134

Pronghorn
Antilocapridae 140

Cattle, Antelope, Sheep,
and Goats/Bovidae 141

Horses and Donkeys
Equidae 144

Glossary

ADAPTABLE: Able to change to adjust to a new situation

ANTLERS: A bony structure that grows from the head of a member of the deer family

BREACH: In whales, a leap out of the water

BURROW: A hole or tunnel in the ground made by an animal

CACHE: A place where an animal stores extra food to be eaten later

CANINE: Belonging to the dog family; also, a pointed tooth

COTERIE: In prairie dogs, a family group

DEWCLAW: Small claws higher up on the leg

DEWLAP: A loose fold of skin hanging from an animal's neck

DIAPHRAGM: A muscle that separates the chest and stomach areas in mammals

ECHOLOCATION: A method for finding a distant object by bouncing sound waves off the object

ENDANGERED: In danger of becoming extinct

ENDOTHERMIC: Having a warm and steady body temperature

EXTINCT: No longer existing

FERAL: Having escaped from being cared for by people and become wild

FOREFOOT: One of the front feet in an animal with four feet

FUNGUS: An organism, such as a mold or mushroom, that must live on a plant, animal, or decaying material

GLAND: An organ in the body that makes a substance that the body can use or release

GRIZZLED: Mixed or streaked with gray

HABITAT: The place or environment where an animal normally lives

HIBERNACULA: Winter shelters for hibernating animals

HIBERNATE: To spend the winter in a resting state, in which the heart rate and body temperature drops

HIND FOOT: One of the back feet in an animal with four feet

HOARY: Having gray or white hair

INCISOR: A sharp-edged front tooth

LITTER: In animals, a group of babies born at one time

MAMMAL: An endothermic animal with a backbone that feeds its young with milk and has body hair

MARSUPIAL: A mammal that carries its young in a pouch

MEMBRANE: A thin, soft layer of animal tissue

MIGRATE: To travel regularly from one region to another to feed or breed

MONOGAMOUS: Having only one mate for a period of time

MONOTREME: An order of egg-laying mammals, including platypuses and echidnas

NOCTURNAL: Active at night

OLD WORLD: Countries in the Eastern Hemisphere, especially European countries

OXYGEN: A gas found in the air that is needed for life

PLACENTAL MAMMAL: A mammal that develops its babies inside its body

PREDATOR: An animal that survives by hunting and eating other animals

RANGE: The region in which an animal lives

ROOST: A place where winged animals gather and rest

RUNWAY: A beaten-down path made by animals

SCUTE: A bony plate or scale on the outside of an animal's body

SPECIES: A group of closely related animals that can breed with one another. A classification level just below genus.

STOTTING: Jumping into the air on four stiff legs

SUBSPECIES: A subgroup of a species that usually lives in a particular region and shares similar characteristics

TERRITORIAL: Showing behavior linked to defending a territory

TERRITORY: An area that is used and defended by an animal or group of animals

THREATENED: Facing threats to survival; likely to become endangered

TORPOR: A sleeplike state in which the body's functions slow down

VENOMOUS: Able to make venom, a poison that animals inject by biting or stinging

VERTEBRATE: An animal with a backbone

ARCTIC FOX KIT p. 104

FIND OUT MORE

WANT TO FIND OUT EVEN MORE
about mammals? Check out these
books, websites, apps, and movies.
Be sure to ask an adult to help
you search the internet to find
the sites below.

Books

Eyewitness Explorer: Nature Ranger.
DK Children, 2015.

Grassy, John. *Mammals (National
Audubon Society First Field Guide).*
Scholastic, 1998.

Kavanagh, James. *Animal Tracks.*
Waterford Press, 2000.

*National Geographic Book of
Mammals.* National Geographic,
1998.

Spelman, Lucy. *National Geographic
Animal Encyclopedia.* National
Geographic, 2012.

Turner, Alan. *National Geographic
Prehistoric Mammals.* National
Geographic, 2004.

Websites

Animal Diversity Web
animaldiversity.org

Animal Fact Guide
animalfactguide.com/
animal-facts/

Bat Conservation International
batcon.org

Easy Science for Kids
easyscienceforkids.com/animals/
mammals/

National Geographic Kids
kids.nationalgeographic.com/
animals/hubs/mammals/

National Wildlife Federation
nwf.org/Educational-Resources/
Wildlife-Guide/Mammals

San Diego Zoo Kids (San Diego Zoo)
kids.sandiegozoo.org

Apps

iNaturalist, LLC: iNaturalist

MyNature: Animal Tracks

National Audubon Society:
Mammals

National Parks Conservation
Association: Park Wildlife

Movies and Documentary Series

BBC: *Planet Earth*

BBC: *Planet Earth II*

BBC and Discovery Channel:
The Life of Mammals

DisneyNature: *Bears*

Index

Boldface indicates illustrations.

Credits

Since 1888, the National Geographic Society has funded more than 12,000 research, exploration, and preservation projects around the world. The Society receives funds from National Geographic Partners, LLC, funded in part by your purchase. A portion of the proceeds from this book supports this vital work. To learn more, visit natgeo.com/info.

NATIONAL GEOGRAPHIC and Yellow Border Design are trademarks of the National Geographic Society, used under license.

For more information, visit nationalgeographic.com, call 1-800-647-5463, or write to the following address:

National Geographic Partners
1145 17th Street N.W.
Washington, D.C. 20036-4688 U.S.A.

Visit us online at nationalgeographic.com/books

For librarians and teachers:
ngchildrensbooks.org

More for kids from National Geographic:
natgeokids.com

National Geographic Kids magazine inspires children to explore their world with fun yet educational articles on animals, science, nature, and more. Using fresh storytelling and amazing photography, Nat Geo Kids shows kids ages 6 to 14 the fascinating truth about the world—and why they should care. **kids.nationalgeographic .com/subscribe**

For information about special discounts for bulk purchases, please contact National Geographic Books Special Sales: specialsales@natgeo.com

For rights or permissions inquiries, please contact National Geographic Books Subsidiary Rights: bookrights@natgeo.com

Designed by Carol Farrar Norton

National Geographic supports K–12 educators with ELA Common Core Resources. Visit natgeoed.org/commoncore for more information.

Library of Congress Cataloging-in-Publication Data

Names: National Geographic Kids (Firm)
Title: Mammals / by National Geographic Kids.
Other titles: Ultimate explorer field guide.
Description: Washington, DC : National Geographic Kids, [2019] | Series: Ultimate explorer field guide | Audience: Ages 8-12. | Audience: Grades 4 to 6. | Includes index.
Identifiers: LCCN 2018031416| ISBN 9781426333699 (pbk.) | ISBN 9781426333705 (hardcover)
Subjects: LCSH: Mammals--Juvenile literature.
Classification: LCC QL706.2 .M283 2019 | DDC 599--dc23
LC record available at https://lccn.loc.gov/2018031416

National Geographic Partners, LLC, and Potomac Global Media, LLC, would like to thank the following members of the project team: Kevin Mulroy, Barbara Brownell Grogan, Matt Propert, Uliana Bazar, Dr. Sam Zeveloff, Jane Sunderland, and Tim Griffin. And from National Geographic Partners: Angela Modany, associate editor; Callie Broaddus, senior designer; Shannon Hibbert, senior photo editor; Joan Gossett, production editor; Anne LeongSon and Gus Tello, production assistants.

Printed in China
18/RRDS/1